# POWER ENGLISH

## BASIC LANGUAGE SKILLS FOR ADULTS

**9**

### Dorothy Rubin
TRENTON STATE COLLEGE

**Editorial supervision:** Timothy Foote
**Production supervision:** Alan Gold
**Manufacturing buyers:** Mike Woerner and Ray Keating

ISBN  0-13-688524-1
Printed in the United States of America
7 8 9 10 11 12     07 06 05 04 03

1-800-321-3106
www.pearsonlearning.com

# CONTENTS

# TO THE TEACHER

*Power English: Basic Language Skills for Adults* is a ten-book series dedicated to helping adults at the ABE level develop their skills in usage, sentence structure, mechanics, and composition. *Power English* consists of the locator test for the series, eight text/workbooks, and this series review book, *Power English 9*.

In this book there are eight Reviews, one for each of the text/workbooks. The Reviews are structured just like the Posttests in the instructional books. For example, the *Power English 1* Review covers the same sixteen topics, with the same number of items, as the Posttest in the text/workbook *Power English 1*. As in the text/workbooks, the Answers section is at the back of this book on perforated pages.

*Power English 9* can be used in any of a variety of ways:

- Any Review can be used as a second posttest for the book to which it relates. Some students may complete a text/workbook but study certain lessons in it a second time. They may then take the appropriate Review and compare their scores on it to those they earned earlier on the Posttest.

- Reviews can be used as reinforcement exercises. For example, students who are working through their second *Power English* text/workbook may interrupt themselves at any point and take the Review for the previous book.

- Reviews can be used to corroborate what the Locator Tests says about students' placement in the *Power English* program. If the Locator Tests say a student should begin to study in *Power English 4,* that student should be able to score well on the *Power English 3* Review in this book.

- If a student begins using *Power English* and later must interrupt his or her course of study for an extended period of time, the Reviews can be used to find where that student should reenter the program.

Your students' unique needs may suggest other uses for the Reviews in this book. You will reap maximum benefit from this book if you think of it as a versatile tool that you can use in a variety of ways in a number of situations.

# POWER ENGLISH

## CAPITAL LETTERS

Write the following sentences over. Use capital letters correctly.

1. mr. and mrs. michael a. pardini are going on a trip in march.

   _____

2. on thursday maria and i are visiting our friend mrs. matthews.

   _____

3. i like the months april, may, and june the best.

   _____

4. herbert k. king and i are leaving in august.

   _____

5. miss sally a. daniels and i start work on monday.

   _____

## TELLING AND ASKING SENTENCES

Write the following sentences over. Use correct capital letters and end marks.

1. what did he say

   _____

2. no one is here

   _____

3. i refused to go there yesterday

   _____

4. did you see that

   _____

5. the poor man is hurt

   _____

GO ON TO THE NEXT PAGE

## WORD ORDER IN SENTENCES

Write the following groups of words over. Write sentences that make sense. Put the words in correct order.

1. Party a my going friends are to.

   _____

2. Far your is house how it to?

   _____

3. Work like you do your?

   _____

4. Child the lost poor is?

   _____

5. Man dance Meg for asked handsome a the.

   _____

## NAMING WORDS (NOUNS)

Fill in each blank with a noun from this list. Use each noun **only once**. Be sure the completed sentences make sense.

NOUN LIST

| children | clothes | house | husband | job |
|----------|---------|-------|---------|-----|
| money | months | school | state | work |

My _____(1)_____ is out of _____(2)_____ . He has been without a _____(3)_____ for three _____(4)_____ . I have a part-time one. It gets me out of the _____(5)_____ . I do not bring home a lot of _____(6)_____ . Our _____(7)_____ need new _____(8)_____ for _____(9)_____ . We may have to move to another _____(10)_____ .

GO ON TO THE NEXT PAGE

## RECOGNIZING NAMING WORDS (NOUNS)

Draw a line under each naming word, or noun, in the following sentences.

1. The child saw the robber leave the store.

2. My brother eats good food only.

3. Her father is my brother.

4. My aunt is a very nice person.

5. The people moved quickly.

## MORE THAN ONE (PLURAL)

Write any naming word, or noun, over that is not correct. Put a **C** in the blank if the naming word is correct.

1. three peach    _____     6. two branch    _____

2. a cookies    _____     7. five crash    _____

3. four camp    _____     8. two pitchers    _____

4. one name    _____     9. ten rose    _____

5. two Jones    _____     10. two Charles    _____

## RECOGNIZING ACTION WORDS (VERBS)

Draw a line under the action word, or verb, in each sentence.

1. The mean man hit the child very hard.

2. We called the police.

3. The man threw the child to the ground.

4. Some of my friends yelled at the man.

5. An angry woman kicked the man.

## ACTION WORDS (VERBS)

Circle the verb that completes each sentence correctly.

1. James and Margie (**dries** or **dry**) dishes together.

2. Pauline (**drive** or **drives**) her car too fast.

GO ON TO THE NEXT PAGE

3. Carl and Franz (**needs** or **need**) help.

4. My friend (**live** or **lives**) near here.

5. My dog (**run** or **runs**) away all the time.

## ACTION WORDS (VERBS): NOW AND BEFORE NOW

Circle each correct action word, or verb.

1. Nurses (**work** or **worked**) hard every day.

2. Rhonda (**plays** or **played**) tennis well yesterday.

3. My dog (**barks** or **barked**) at a cat a moment ago.

4. She (**loves** or **loved**) her boyfriend now.

5. Diego and I (**need** or **needed**) one more ticket for last week's game.

## THE WORDS *AM, ARE,* AND *IS*

Fill in each blank with **am**, **are**, or **is**.

1. They _____ not very nice people.

2. I _____ happy now.

3. _____ she your friend?

4. We _____ both on strike.

5. Richard and Dina _____ here.

## ACTION WORDS AND HELPING WORDS (VERBS)

Fill in each blank with **am**, **are**, or **is**.

1. George and I _____ running for office.

2. I _____ running for mayor.

3. _____ you going to vote for me?

4. My aunt _____ voting for me.

5. She _____ helping me get votes.

GO ON TO THE NEXT PAGE

## THE WORDS *HE, SHE, IT, I,* AND *THEY*

Fill in each blank with **he**, **she**, **it**, **I**, or **they**.

1. Felipe joined the army.

   _____ wanted to leave home.

2. Stephen, Irene, and Seth are playing in a band.

   _____ are very good.

3. My girlfriend likes to dance with me.

   _____ and _____ dance well together.

4. Carol and Sharon are good friends.

   _____ do many things together.

5. The cat got stuck in the tree.

   _____ was too frightened to climb down.

## RECOGNIZING DESCRIBING WORDS (ADJECTIVES)

Draw a line under every word that describes a naming word.

1. Today there is a beautiful blue sky.

2. The large gray cat drank its cold milk.

3. My charming friend drives too fast.

4. The frightened woman screamed loudly.

5. My pretty red coat has a black collar.

## THE WORDS *A* AND *AN*

Write **a** or **an** in front of the following words.

1. _____ old house

2. _____ sharp knife

3. _____ hard worker

4. _____ yellow sweater

5. _____ easy problem

6. _____ young child

7. _____ oak tree

8. _____ action

9. _____ cute baby

10. _____ even score

GO ON TO THE NEXT PAGE

5

## WRITING A FRIENDLY LETTER

Write a friendly letter to a friend. Tell him or her that you had a nice time at his or her house. Use today's date. End the letter with your name.

```
                                        _____ ____, 19____

    Dear _____,

    _____

    _____

    _____

                          Your friend,

                          _____
```

## THE ALPHABET

Write these 26 words in alphabetical order.

| x-ray | enter | book | milk | seven | quiet | help | jam | very |
|-------|-------|------|------|-------|-------|------|-----|------|
| ice | tree | was | ran | all | fry | no | out | zoo |
| park | girl | carrot | kit | year | love | dark | use | |

1. _____      10. _____      19. _____

2. _____      11. _____      20. _____

3. _____      12. _____      21. _____

4. _____      13. _____      22. _____

5. _____      14. _____      23. _____

6. _____      15. _____      24. _____

7. _____      16. _____      25. _____

8. _____      17. _____      26. _____

9. _____      18. _____

**STOP** CHECK ANSWERS BEGINNING ON PAGE 117.

Count how many items you answered correctly in each **Section** of the Review. Write your score per section in the **My Scores** column. If all your section scores are as high as the **Good Scores**, go on to the next stage of your study in *Power English*. If any of your section scores are lower than the **Good Scores**, study the lessons on the assigned **Review Pages** in *Power English 1* again before you go on.

| Section | Good Scores | My Scores | Review Pages |
|---|---|---|---|
| Capital Letters | 4 or 5 | | 2–3, 22–23, 42, 64, 88–89 |
| Telling and Asking Sentences | 4 or 5 | | 4–6, 24–26, 43, 65–66, 90 |
| Word Order in Sentences | 4 or 5 | | 28–29, 44, 67, 91 |
| Naming Words (Nouns) | 8, 9, or 10 | | 8, 30, 45, 70, 94 |
| Recognizing Naming Words (Nouns) | 4 or 5 | | 9, 31, 46 |
| More Than One (Plural) | 8, 9, or 10 | | 10–11, 32–33, 47, 71, 95 |
| Recognizing Action Words (Verbs) | 4 or 5 | | 13, 35 |
| Action Words (Verbs) | 4 or 5 | | 12, 34, 54, 74, 99 |
| Action Words (Verbs): Now and Before Now | 4 or 5 | | 76–77, 101 |

| Section | Good Scores | My Scores | Review Pages |
| --- | --- | --- | --- |
| The Words **Am**, **Are**, and **Is** | 4 or 5 | | 52–53 |
| Action Words and Helping Words (Verbs) | 4 or 5 | | 55, 75, 100 |
| The Words **He**, **She**, **It**, **I**, and **They** | 4 or 5 | | 48–49, 72, 96–97 |
| Recognizing Describing Words (Adjectives) | 4 or 5 | | 50–51, 73, 98 |
| The Words **A** and **An** | 8, 9, or 10 | | 14 |
| Writing a Friendly Letter | A correct letter | | 78, 102 |
| The Alphabet | All correct | | 15–16, 36, 56, 79, 103 |

## CAPITALIZING

Write the following sentences over. Capitalize correctly. Remember to underline book titles and to put quotation marks around short story titles.

1. in january tomiko and i are going to chicago, illinois.

   _____

2. i love to read stories like "killer in the night."

   _____

3. <u>power english</u> helps people gain writing skills.

   _____

4. in may sara is moving to hardy drive in baltimore, maryland.

   _____

5. i just finished reading <u>a trip to the moon</u>.

   _____

## TELLING AND ASKING SENTENCES

Write the following over. Capitalize and add end marks correctly.

1. mr. and mrs. torres enjoy reading

   _____

2. who said that to you

   _____

3. that is an incredible thing to say

   _____

4. what do they want

   _____

5. don't go

   _____

GO ON TO THE NEXT PAGE

## ASKING SENTENCES (QUESTIONS)

Write a question to go with each telling sentence.

**1.** I read at night.

_____

**2.** Ben lives on Seventh Avenue.

_____

**3.** I ride the bus to work.

_____

**4.** Bernice moved to New York City in July.

_____

**5.** Leon loves to play tennis.

_____

## END MARKS

Put the correct end mark at the end of each sentence.

**1.** She is a very special person

**2.** I can't believe you did that

**3.** Who saw them go

**4.** This is incredible

**5.** Help them

## RECOGNIZING SENTENCES

Put a check (√) by each of the sentences.

☐ **1.** Before that is.

☐ **2.** My best friend.

☐ **3.** Do that now.

☐ **4.** Run faster.

☐ **5.** From here to the store.

GO ON TO THE NEXT PAGE

## SENTENCE PARTS

Find the words from Group Two, the predicate, that go with each complete subject from Group One. Write the letter in the blank.

| GROUP ONE (COMPLETE SUBJECT) | GROUP TWO (PREDICATE) |
|---|---|
| ____ 1. A house | a. were working hard to free her. |
| ____ 2. A poor child | b. was terrible to watch. |
| ____ 3. People | c. were on top of the child. |
| ____ 4. Bricks and wood | d. was trapped. |
| ____ 5. It | e. had fallen. |

## WORD ORDER IN SENTENCES

Use the following groups of words to write sentences.

1. Loved needs to everyone be.

_____

2. Alone world all Christine the in is.

_____

3. Invites one ever her no dinner to.

_____

4. Morning work goes the in she to.

_____

5. Apartment home every she night comes an empty to.

_____

## THE COMPLETE SUBJECT OF A SENTENCE

Put a line under the complete subject in each sentence.

1. Ellen and Laura enjoy walking in the woods.

2. The trees are losing their leaves.

3. My sisters and brothers are making a party for me.

4. Tara and I have lots to do.

5. They wanted to leave the store.

GO ON TO THE NEXT PAGE

**MORE THAN ONE (PLURAL)**

The following nouns are not correct. Write each one over correctly in the blank.

1. two box _____
2. three baby _____
3. ten wash _____
4. four hobby _____
5. five way _____

6. five boy _____
7. six ax _____
8. two dummy _____
9. four door _____
10. two pass _____

**THE PRONOUNS *I, YOU, HE, SHE, IT, WE,* AND *THEY***

Fill in the blanks with **I, you, he, she, it, we,** or **they**. Use each pronoun **once only**.

The man looked sick. _____ was walking very slowly. A dog
                              (1)

barked at the man. _____ started to run after the man. The poor
                        (2)

man looked scared.

My friends and _____ were coming home from school.
                      (3)

_____ saw the man and the dog. The dog was growling at the
      (4)

man. Some other people also saw the dog and the man. _____
                                                              (5)

stopped to help the man.

**RECOGNIZING DESCRIBING WORDS (ADJECTIVES)**

Draw a line under each of the describing words, or adjectives.

1. I hate to throw out old broken things.

2. I keep worn, rusty tools and large boxes of junk.

3. My nice apartment is filled with useless things.

4. My wife hates to keep silly, unused things.

5. I may have to throw out my biggest box of junk.

GO ON TO THE NEXT PAGE

## DESCRIBING WORDS (ADJECTIVES)

In each sentence, find the describing word, or adjective, that is used to compare. In the blank, write the describing word over correctly. Add the **er** or **est** ending.

1. The large dog I ever saw wagged its tail.          _____

2. That is the sloppy desk of all.                     _____

3. Luiz is always merry than David.                    _____

4. This lake is deep than the other one.               _____

5. That is the lazy dog of any I have ever seen.       _____

## ACTION WORDS (VERBS)

The verbs in the following sentences are not correct. Write the correct verbs in the blanks.

1. My brothers always argues at big dinners.           _____

2. My mother usually speak softly.                     _____

3. We all yells at one another.                        _____

4. Then my father raise his voice.                     _____

5. We makes my mother very sad.                        _____

## ACTION WORDS (VERBS): PRESENT, PAST, AND FUTURE TIME

Write the correct action words in the blanks in these sentences.

1. I _____ all the time now. (**hurry, hurried, will hurry**)

2. The men _____ to work earlier. (**rush, rushed, will rush**)

3. My child _____ shoes today. (**needs, needed, will need**)

4. The plane _____ soon. (**lands, landed, will land**)

5. José _____ to help them before. (**tries, tried, will try**)

GO ON TO THE NEXT PAGE

## THE WORDS *AM, ARE, IS, WAS,* AND *WERE* (VERBS)

Fill in each blank with the words **am**, **are**, **is**, **was**, or **were**.

1. I _____ not happy about that now.

2. _____ you at the meeting yesterday?

3. Pina and Carmen _____ there now.

4. _____ the meeting a good one yesterday?

5. My boss _____ nice to me these days.

## THE WORDS *THERE IS* AND *THERE ARE*

Fill in the blanks with **There is** or **There are**.

1. _____ my sweater.

2. _____ my friends now.

3. _____ the bus stop.

4. _____ the things we need.

5. _____ the ocean.

## THE WORDS *HAS, HAD,* AND *HAVE* (VERBS)

Fill in each blank with **has**, **had**, or **have**.

1. I _____ three children.

2. My husband _____ two jobs now.

3. He and I _____ too much to do every day.

4. Our children _____ jobs now.

5. We _____ many problems last year.

## THE WORDS *DO, DOES,* AND *DID* (VERBS)

Fill in each blank with **do**, **does**, or **did**.

1. Kenji _____ that already.

2. We _____ a lot for him now.

3. _____ that now for me.

4. I _____ the hard work yesterday.

5. He _____ everything very well now.

GO ON TO THE NEXT PAGE

## SHORTENING WORDS (CONTRACTIONS)

Write each pair of words over as one word.

1. will not _____
2. should not _____
3. was not _____
4. is not _____
5. had not _____

6. has not _____
7. do not _____
8. have not _____
9. were not _____
10. are not _____

## THE WORDS *A* AND *AN*

Put **a** or **an** before each of the following words and phrases.

1. _____ happy person
2. _____ orange
3. _____ honest man
4. _____ honor

5. _____ pie
6. _____ iron
7. _____ hour

8. _____ x-ray
9. _____ ocean
10. _____ young woman

## WRITING A FRIENDLY LETTER

Write a letter to thank someone for helping you to do something.

_____ _____, 19_____

Dear _____,

_____

_____

_____

_____

_____

Your pal,

_____

GO ON TO THE NEXT PAGE

## ADDRESSING AN ENVELOPE

Here is an envelope. Address it to a friend. You are the sender of the letter.

_____

_____

_____

        _____

        _____

        _____

## SPELLING

Write the correct word in each blank.

1. I am going _____ the store at _____ o'clock, _____ . (**two—to—too**)

2. Is it _____ to _____ her a letter? (**write—right**)

3. I don't _____ why you have _____ money. (**no—know**)

4. I _____ an apple at _____ o'clock. (**eight—ate**)

5. She can _____ dresses _____ well! (**so—sew**)

6. I did _____ that they were _____ . (**here—hear**)

7. Dan _____ a book about a _____ house. (**read—red**)

GO ON TO THE NEXT PAGE

**8.** Will _____ friend be here in an _____ ?

(**hour—our**)

**9.** I can _____ you after I buy the _____ .

(**meat—meet**)

**10.** He will _____ that on the _____ home.

(**way—weigh**)

## ALPHABETIZING

Write the following groups of words over in alphabetical order. Put commas between the words in the lists you write.

**1.** board, bite, broom, blame, base, bet, busy

_____

**2.** save, cute, frame, bank, blame, slap, cream

_____

**3.** flower, farm, frame, fool, full, feel, fine

_____

**4.** all, are, at, am, able, ask, act

_____

**5.** track, tell, the, time, tune, too, two

_____

**STOP** CHECK ANSWERS BEGINNING ON PAGE 118.

Count how many items you answered correctly in each **Section** of the Review. Write your score per section in the **My Scores** column. If all your section scores are as high as the **Good Scores**, go on to the next stage of your study in *Power English*. If any of your section scores are lower than the **Good Scores**, study the lessons on the assigned **Review Pages** in *Power English 2* again before you go on.

| Section | Good Scores | My Scores | Review Pages |
|---|---|---|---|
| Capitalizing | 4 or 5 | | 2, 24, 46, 68, 88 |
| Telling and Asking Sentences | 4 or 5 | | 3 |
| Asking Sentences (Questions) | 4 or 5 | | 4, 25–26 |
| End Marks | 4 or 5 | | 6, 49, 71, 89 |
| Recognizing Sentences | 4 or 5 | | 29–30, 47, 69 |
| Sentence Parts | 4 or 5 | | 5, 27, 70, 90 |
| Word Order in Sentences | 4 or 5 | | 91 |
| The Complete Subject of a Sentence | 4 or 5 | | 28, 48 |
| More Than One (Plural) | 8, 9, or 10 | | 8, 31, 50, 72 |
| The Pronouns **I**, **You**, **He**, **She**, **It**, **We**, and **They** | 4 or 5 | | 9, 51–52 |
| Recognizing Describing Words (Adjectives) | 4 or 5 | | 32, 53 |
| Describing Words (Adjectives) | 4 or 5 | | 73–74, 92 |
| Action Words (Verbs) | 4 or 5 | | 10 |

| Section | Good Scores | My Scores | Review Pages |
|---|---|---|---|
| Action Words (Verbs): Present, Past, and Future Time | 4 or 5 | | 33–34, 54, 75, 93 |
| The Words **Am, Are, Is, Was,** and **Were** (Verbs) | 4 or 5 | | 11–12 |
| The Words **There is** and **There are** | 4 or 5 | | 35 |
| The Words **Has, Had,** and **Have** (Verbs) | 4 or 5 | | 36–37, 55–56 |
| The Words **Do, Does,** and **Did** (Verbs) | 4 or 5 | | 76–77, 94–95 |
| Shortening Words (Contractions) | 8, 9, or 10 | | 13, 78 |
| The Words **A** and **An** | 8, 9, or 10 | | 14, 79, 96 |
| Writing a Friendly Letter | A correct letter | | 97–98 |
| Addressing an Envelope | Both addresses correct | | 57, 99 |
| Spelling | 8, 9, or 10 | | 59, 80, 100 |
| Alphabetizing | 4 or 5 | | 15, 38, 60, 81, 101 |

**CAPITALIZING**

Write the following sentences over. Capitalize correctly. Put quotation marks around short story and poem titles.

1. mr. and mrs. a. i. adams live on spruce street in reno, nevada.

   _____

2. miss jasper and ms. veldez are going to england in the summer.

   _____

3. "i am on a free ride to nowhere" is an interesting story.

   _____

4. maria likes funny love poems like "my heart is a marshmallow."

   _____

5. mr. and mrs. j. l. zavarelli have lived in texas, virginia, utah, oregon, and maine.

   _____

**COMPOUND SUBJECTS AND VERBS IN SENTENCES**

Draw one line under each noun in the complete subject in each sentence. Draw two lines under each verb in each sentence.

1. Marcos and Tony quit work and traveled west.

2. The two young men and their dog headed toward California.

3. In Reno they gambled and lost most of their money.

4. A kind man and his wife offered Tony and Marcos a ride to California.

5. The four people sang songs and joked all the way to California.

GO ON TO THE NEXT PAGE

## SENTENCE PARTS

Find the words from Group Two, the predicate, that go with each complete subject from Group One. Write the letter in the blank.

GROUP ONE (COMPLETE SUBJECT)

____ 1. Travel

____ 2. I

____ 3. My job

____ 4. Many people

____ 5. They

GROUP TWO (PREDICATE)

a. requires me to travel.

b. love to travel.

c. should have my job.

d. am not a good traveler.

e. makes me ill.

## RECOGNIZING SENTENCES

Put a check (√) by the sentences.

☐ 1. Help is on the way.

☐ 2. Go immediately.

☐ 3. Several doctors and nurses.

☐ 4. After the meeting is.

☐ 5. Ray and his wife Liza.

## COMBINING SENTENCES

Write one sentence that combines each set of three sentences.

1. Robert needs help now.
   Robert wants help now.
   Robert has help now.

   _____

2. Sara types well.
   Sara writes well.
   Sara speaks well.

   _____

GO ON TO THE NEXT PAGE

22

**3.** The lake looks good.
The lake feels good.
The lake smells good.

_____

**4.** Clara cleans the house.
Clara goes to work.
Clara takes care of the children.

_____

**5.** The movie bothered us.
The movie frightened us.
The movie drained us.

_____

## SHORTENING SENTENCES WITH COMMAS

Write the following sentences over. Shorten them by using commas.

**1.** Richard works hard every day and Florence works hard every day and Julio works hard every day.

_____

**2.** José usually eats too much at Thanksgiving and Maria usually eats too much at Thanksgiving and Francis usually eats too much at Thanksgiving.

_____

**3.** Karen entered the new store and Stanley entered the new store and I entered the new store.

_____

**4.** The small child is here now and the small dog is here now and the small kitten is here now.

_____

**5.** The new salesperson started work on Monday and the new boss started work on Monday and the new secretary started work on Monday.

_____

GO ON TO THE NEXT PAGE

## WORD ORDER IN SENTENCES AND COMMAS

Use the following groups of words to write sentences. Add necessary commas.

1. And Stephanie here Dennis work I.

   _____

2. Fat and butter red in cream are meat high.

   _____

3. Swimming love bowling I and walking.

   _____

4. The ate we and sandwiches party at salads fruit.

   _____

5. His escaped police friend an looking the are prisoner wife for and his.

   _____

## COMMAND SENTENCES

Put the correct end mark at the end of each sentence.

1. Don't go there

2. Wait

3. Who said that

4. Walter is very mean

5. Hurry up

## RECOGNIZING NAMING WORDS (NOUNS)

Draw a line under each of the nouns in the following short story.

I finally met a person I could fall in love with. However, my luck, he is already married. I will not go out with a married man. He likes me. However, he has a wife. I would not like a woman to do the same thing to me if I were married. He has asked me for dates. It's hard, but I keep saying "No." Why are all the good men married? It is hard being a single woman today.

GO ON TO THE NEXT PAGE

**MORE THAN ONE (PLURAL)**

Write the plural of each of the following nouns.

1. child _____   6. foot _____
2. man _____   7. woman _____
3. tooth _____   8. mouse _____
4. goose _____   9. book _____
5. baby _____   10. glass _____

**THE PRONOUNS *I*, *YOU*, *HE*, *SHE*, *IT*, *WE*, AND *THEY***

Fill in each blank with **I**, **you**, **he**, **she**, **it**, **we**, or **they**.

1. Life has its ups and downs.

   _____ can be difficult at times.

2. The workers voted to strike.

   _____ really didn't want to do this.

3. My father and I work for the same company.

   _____ would both be out of work.

4. My father is a very stubborn man.

   _____ never changes his mind.

5. My father likes to work with me.

   _____ also like to work with him.

**THE PRONOUNS *HIM* AND *HER***

Fill in each blank with the correct word.

1. This is for _____. (**he** or **him**)

2. _____ is a very nice person. (**Her** or **She**)

3. Is this about _____? (**he** or **him**)

4. I am not against _____. (**she** or **her**)

5. What did you say about _____? (**he** or **him**)

GO ON TO THE NEXT PAGE

## THE PRONOUN *THEM*

Fill in each blank with **they** or **them**.

1. This is for _____.

2. _____ are not happy about that.

3. Is that about _____?

4. _____ should know better than that.

5. Don't give it to _____.

## DESCRIBING WORDS AND LINKING WORDS

Draw a line under each of the describing words in these sentences.

1. That nice young man is my favorite son-in-law.

2. The older woman looks happy and content.

3. The charming, handsome man is lucky.

4. My big feet are tired.

5. The scary movie was long.

## DESCRIBING WORDS (ADJECTIVES)

In the blank in each sentence, write the describing word with an **er** or **est** ending.

1. Of course, I am _____ than you. (**tall**)

2. Certainly, Eric is the _____ person here. (**smart**)

3. That is the _____ thing she has ever said. (**stupid**)

4. She is _____ than he. (**nice**)

5. Ruth is the _____ person I know. (**lovely**)

## ACTION WORDS (VERBS)

In the blanks, write the past and future forms of each verb.

|  | PAST TIME | FUTURE TIME |
| --- | --- | --- |
| 1. climb | _____ | _____ |
| 2. bake | _____ | _____ |

GO ON TO THE NEXT PAGE

|            | PAST TIME | FUTURE TIME |
|------------|-----------|-------------|
| **3.** cook | _____ | _____ |
| **4.** work | _____ | _____ |
| **5.** wash | _____ | _____ |

## THE VERBS *GO, GOES, WENT,* AND *WILL GO*

Fill in each blank with **go**, **goes**, **went**, or **will go**.

1. I _____ there tomorrow.

2. Bridget and I _____ to the movies yesterday.

3. She _____ to work now.

4. They _____ with us to the store just before.

5. Time _____ too fast for me now.

## THE VERBS *HAS, HAVE, HAD,* AND *WILL HAVE*

Fill in each blank with **has**, **have**, **had**, or **will have**.

1. _____ it ready for me by this afternoon.

2. They _____ time to think about it later.

3. Our bus _____ a flat tire before.

4. He _____ no ride to work now.

5. The Adamses _____ lots of money soon.

## THE VERBS *DO, DOES, DID,* AND *WILL DO*

Fill in each blank with **do**, **does**, **did**, or **will do**.

1. I _____ that already.

2. We _____ many things together now.

3. Adam and Emily _____ everything later.

4. They _____ a lot yesterday.

5. The workers _____ well now.

GO ON TO THE NEXT PAGE

## THE VERBS *SEE*, *SEES*, *SAW*, AND *WILL SEE*

Fill in each blank with **see**, **sees**, **saw**, or **will see**.

1. He _____ you soon.

2. My boss _____ me at the mall yesterday.

3. I _____ better now with my new glasses.

4. The fielder _____ the ball too late that time.

5. He _____ us now.

## RECOGNIZING DESCRIBING WORDS (ADVERBS)

Draw a line under each adverb.

1. My young children run fast.

2. Our large family went to the sandy beach yesterday.

3. The hot sun was shining brightly.

4. My poor head and burned body hurt terribly.

5. I begged my nice family to leave immediately.

## DESCRIBING WORDS (ADVERBS)

Change the following adjectives into adverbs by adding an **ly** ending.
Double the final consonant if necessary.

1. terrible _____

2. nice _____

3. quick _____

4. careful _____

5. cruel _____

6. horrible _____

7. cheerful _____

8. slow _____

9. happy _____

10. sad _____

## WRITING THE TIME OF DAY

Write each time in numbers with **A.M.** or **P.M.**

1. Ten past two in the morning _____

2. Five past nine at night _____

3. Twenty past three in the afternoon _____

4. A quarter past eleven in the morning _____

5. Half-past eight at night _____

GO ON TO THE NEXT PAGE

## WRITING DATES

Write the following dates correctly.

1. august 10 1929      _____

2. june 3 1988      _____

3. february 11 1954      _____

4. october 10 1955      _____

5. may 4 1952      _____

## WRITING ADDRESSES

Write each of the following addresses correctly.

1. 912 carter road

   chicago illinois 60610

   _____

   _____

2. 213 main street

   syracuse new york 13220

   _____

   _____

## SHORTENING WORDS (CONTRACTIONS)

Write each word or pair of words over as a contraction.

1. cannot _____

2. I will _____

3. they are _____

4. I am _____

5. we have _____

6. have not _____

7. she has _____

8. could not _____

9. he is _____

10. will not _____

## THE WORDS A AND AN

Put **a** or **an** before each of the following words.

1. _____ honest person

2. _____ hour

3. _____ unusual sight

4. _____ early date

5. _____ union

6. _____ empire

7. _____ house

8. _____ usual thing

9. _____ happy child

10. _____ ugly picture

GO ON TO THE NEXT PAGE

## USING *YES* AND *NO* IN A SENTENCE

Write the following sentences over. Capitalize and add necessary commas.

1. yes i will help you.

   _____

2. no he is not here now.

   _____

3. yes they were here earlier.

   _____

4. yes i know them well.

   _____

5. no i do not like them.

   _____

## WRITING AN INVITATION

Use the following form to invite someone to a party at your house.

_____

GO ON TO THE NEXT PAGE

## ADDRESSING AN ENVELOPE

Here is an envelope. Address it to the person you invited to your party.

_____

_____

_____

                    _____

                    _____

                    _____

## SPELLING

In the blanks, write each word with an **ing** ending and with an **ed** ending.

|  | **ING** ENDING | **ED** ENDING |
| --- | --- | --- |
| 1. hope | _____ | _____ |
| 2. can | _____ | _____ |
| 3. trap | _____ | _____ |
| 4. jump | _____ | _____ |
| 5. drop | _____ | _____ |
| 6. hop | _____ | _____ |
| 7. pin | _____ | _____ |
| 8. look | _____ | _____ |
| 9. chop | _____ | _____ |
| 10. dine | _____ | _____ |

GO ON TO THE NEXT PAGE

## SPELLING

These sentences have misspelled words. They do not make sense. Write each sentence over so that it makes sense. Spell each word correctly.

1. The fare man said he did not have any bus fair.

   _____

2. I do not no if that is the right weigh to the fare.

   _____

## ALPHABETIZING

Write the following names in alphabetical order. Put commas between the names in the list you write.

Sally Dryer     Joseph Bryant     David Foyer     Sara Dreber     Tara Driem
Francis Cruel     Edward Donne     George Doll     Kathy Drum     Allan Brandeis
Dorothy Drome     Alice Cracker     Sylvia Dram     Julio Droom     Frank Dorm

_____

_____

_____

_____

_____

## ALPHABETIZING (USING THE DICTIONARY)

Use the guide words **drain** and **dry** to answer the questions. Write **Yes** or **No** in each blank.

1. Is the word **drive** on this page? _____

2. Is the word **drove** on this page? _____

3. Is the word **drip** on this page? _____

4. Is the word **drum** on this page? _____

5. Is the word **deep** on this page? _____

**STOP** CHECK ANSWERS BEGINNING ON PAGE 119.

Count how many items you answered correctly in each **Section** of the Review. Write your score per section in the **My Scores** column. If all your section scores are as high as the **Good Scores**, go on to the next stage of your study in *Power English*. If any of your section scores are lower than the **Good Scores**, study the lessons on the assigned **Review Pages** in *Power English 3* again before you go on.

| Section | Good Scores | My Scores | Review Pages |
|---|---|---|---|
| Capitalizing | 4 or 5 | | 2, 22, 44–45, 68, 98 |
| Compound Subjects and Verbs in Sentences | 4 or 5 | | 23 |
| Sentence Parts | 4 or 5 | | 5, 46 |
| Recognizing Sentences | 4 or 5 | | 25 |
| Combining Sentences | 4 or 5 | | 71, 99–100 |
| Shortening Sentences with Commas | 4 or 5 | | 47, 48, 72, 73–74, 101, 102 |
| Word Order in Sentences and Commas | 4 or 5 | | 49 |
| Command Sentences | 4 or 5 | | 26 |
| Recognizing Naming Words (Nouns) | 8, 9, or 10 | | 50 |
| More Than One (Plural) | 8, 9, or 10 | | 6 |
| The Pronouns **I**, **You**, **He**, **She**, **It**, **We**, and **They** | 4 or 5 | | 27, 28 |
| The Pronouns **Him** and **Her** | 4 or 5 | | 76 |
| The Pronoun **Them** | 4 or 5 | | 108 |
| Describing Words and Linking Words | 4 or 5 | | 103–104 |
| Describing Words (Adjectives) | 4 or 5 | | 7 |

| Section | Good Scores | My Scores | Review Pages |
|---|---|---|---|
| Action Words (Verbs) | 4 or 5 | | 8 |
| The Verbs **Go**, **Goes**, **Went**, and **Will Go** | 4 or 5 | | 51, 52 |
| The Verbs **Has**, **Have**, **Had**, and **Will Have** | 4 or 5 | | 29 |
| The Verbs **Do**, **Does**, **Did**, and **Will Do** | 4 or 5 | | 9 |
| The Verbs **See**, **Sees**, **Saw**, and **Will See** | 4 or 5 | | 30, 31 |
| Recognizing Describing Words (Adverbs) | 4 or 5 | | 10 |
| Describing Words (Adverbs) | 8, 9, or 10 | | 11, 53, 75, 105 |
| Writing the Time of Day | 4 or 5 | | 57, 109, 110 |
| Writing Dates | 4 or 5 | | 81 |
| Writing Addresses | 2 | | 55–56 |
| Shortening Words (Contractions) | 8, 9, or 10 | | 12, 13, 32, 77–78 |
| The Words **A** and **An** | 8, 9, or 10 | | 33, 54 |
| Using **Yes** and **No** in a Sentence | 4 or 5 | | 79–80 |
| Writing an Invitation | A correct letter | | 82–83, 84–85 |
| Addressing an Envelope | Both addresses correct | | 113 |
| Spelling | 8, 9, or 10 | | 58, 86, 114 |
| Spelling | Correct addresses | | 14, 34 |
| Alphabetizing | All correct | | 15, 35–36, 59, 87–88 |
| Alphabetizing (Using the Dictionary) | 4 or 5 | | 115 |

## CAPITALIZING (COMMON NOUNS AND PROPER NOUNS)

Here is a list of nouns. Correct the nouns that are not written correctly. Put a **C** in the blank by a noun that is correct.

1. Grapes _____
2. atlantic ocean _____
3. Mr. marrero _____
4. Winter _____
5. dave c. ridgley _____
6. memorial day _____
7. Fruit _____
8. halloween _____
9. independence day _____
10. labor day _____

11. ohio _____
12. City _____
13. Teacher _____
14. mayor _____
15. Autumn _____
16. christmas _____
17. Bedroom _____
18. Day _____
19. Number _____
20. Labor _____

## SINGULAR AND PLURAL SUBJECTS

Here is a list of nouns and pronouns from complete subjects. Write **S** in the blank if the subject of the sentence is singular. Write **P** in the blank if the subject of the sentence is plural.

1. safes _____
2. we _____
3. She _____
4. babies _____
5. James L. Davies _____

6. parents _____
7. Fred and I _____
8. children _____
9. worker _____
10. feet _____

GO ON TO THE NEXT PAGE

## SENTENCE PARTS

Find the words from Group Two, the predicate, that go with each complete subject from Group One. Write the letter in the blank.

GROUP ONE (COMPLETE SUBJECT)

_____ 1. There

_____ 2. I

_____ 3. My sister, Patricia,

_____ 4. We all

_____ 5. My parents

GROUP TWO (PREDICATE)

a. have four brothers and one sister.

b. sleeps in the living room.

c. are eight people in my family.

d. work very hard.

e. still live at home.

## RECOGNIZING SENTENCES

Put a check (√) by each of the sentences.

☐ 1. Stop talking.

☐ 2. Into the woods.

☐ 3. Warren Bailey and Claire Trent.

☐ 4. Running around in the park.

☐ 5. Do not go there now.

## WORD ORDER IN SENTENCES

Use the following groups of words to write sentences. Add necessary commas.

1. Sister I work place in brother same and the my.

_____

2. Flowers tulips are roses and favorite pansies my.

_____

## END MARKS

Put the proper end mark at the end of each sentence.

1. Hurry up

2. Stand still

3. Is that the truth

4. Ken tries hard

5. Yes, I will go tomorrow

GO ON TO THE NEXT PAGE

## WRITING SENTENCES WITH COMPOUND SUBJECTS

The complete subjects of two sentences follow. Finish each sentence by writing the predicate.

1. The train and car

   _____

2. The men, women, and children

   _____

## COMBINING SENTENCES

Write one sentence that combines the two sentences in each pair.

1. George won a great battle.
   George found a reason to live.

   _____

2. He had been very ill.
   He had almost given up.

   _____

3. His family supported him.
   His family stayed by him.

   _____

4. They gave him courage.
   They refused to let him die.

   _____

5. George beat all the odds.
   George is now a famous ballplayer.

   _____

GO ON TO THE NEXT PAGE

## COMBINING SENTENCES

Write one sentence that combines the three sentences in each set.

1. Life is precious.
   Life must be lived to its fullest.
   Life should not be wasted.

   _____

   _____

2. Every person needs love.
   Every person needs understanding.
   Every person needs belonging.

   _____

   _____

3. Happiness cannot be bought.
   Love cannot be bought.
   Belonging cannot be bought.

   _____

   _____

4. The small child had fallen in a well.
   The small child had broken her leg.
   The small child had twisted her neck.

   _____

   _____

5. The firemen tried to get the child out of the well.
   The police tried to get the child out of the well.
   The rescue squad tried to get the child out of the well.

   _____

   _____

GO ON TO THE NEXT PAGE

**SHORTENING SENTENCES WITH COMMAS**

Shorten the following sentences using commas.

1. All the letters and all the packages and all the stamps were stolen from the mail carrier.

   _____

   _____

2. Jeff and Marcella and Hideo and I are best friends.

   _____

   _____

3. Peter worked as a delivery boy and as a clerk and as a salesperson.

   _____

   _____

4. The brave man rushed into the burning building and ran up the stairs and rescued the infant.

   _____

   _____

5. The men and the women and the children screamed with joy.

   _____

   _____

**ADJECTIVES (DESCRIBING WORDS)**

In each sentence, find the adjective that is used to compare. In the blank, write the adjective correctly. Add the **er** or **est** ending.

1. That shark is the long one I have ever seen.   _____

2. Jan is not lazy than Wendy.   _____

3. Lan looks healthy than Ana.   _____

4. These walls are the dirty in the building.   _____

5. This room looks the clean of all.   _____

GO ON TO THE NEXT PAGE

## ADJECTIVES (DESCRIBING WORDS) AND LINKING WORDS

Fill in each blank in the sentences with an adjective from the list. Use an adjective **once only**.

ADJECTIVE LIST

cleverest    good    happy    prettier    smarter

1. She is _____ than Linda.

2. Dorotea is _____ than Jeanne.

3. Ali seems _____ with his raise.

4. Henri is the _____ person here.

5. This music sounds _____.

## THE PRONOUNS *I, YOU, HE, SHE, IT, WE,* AND *THEY*

Fill in each blank with **I**, **you**, **he**, **she**, **it**, **we**, or **they**.

1. The wreckers tore down the old building.

   _____ was old and falling apart.

2. My father and I helped tear down the building.

   _____ are city workers.

3. My father told me to be careful.

   _____ listened to him.

4. Last year one man fell off a ladder.

   _____ was very badly hurt.

5. His hard hat protected his head.

   _____ is a safety hat.

## THE PRONOUNS *ME, HIM, HER, US,* AND *THEM*

Fill in each blank with the correct word.

1. Give that to _____. (**him** or **he**)

2. She and _____ are going away together. (**I** or **me**)

3. This is only between you and _____. (**me** or **I**)

4. Who is against _____? (**we** or **us**)

5. _____ look very nice. (**Them** or **They**)

GO ON TO THE NEXT PAGE

## MORE THAN ONE (NOUN PLURALS)

Write the plural of each of the following nouns.

1. shelf _____        6. safe _____

2. wife _____        7. mouse _____

3. table _____        8. cherry _____

4. tooth _____        9. foot _____

5. knife _____        10. loaf _____

## AGREEMENT OF SUBJECT AND VERB

Underline the verb that is correct for the sentence.

1. The snow (**fall** or **falls**) very slowly.

2. It (**look** or **looks**) like a white blanket.

3. I (**love** or **loves**) winter here.

4. My friends (**like** or **likes**) warm weather only.

5. They (**go** or **goes**) to a warmer place in the winter.

## VERBS (ACTION WORDS): PRESENT TIME

Correct the verb in each sentence. In the blank, write the correct present-time verb.

1. She arrive too early most days.        _____

2. The animals plays nicely together.        _____

3. I eats only good food.        _____

4. They does nothing most days.        _____

5. I goes there all the time.        _____

## THE VERBS *RUN, RUNS, RAN,* AND *WILL RUN*

Fill in the blanks with **run**, **runs**, **ran**, or **will run**.

1. The mayor _____ for office again next year.

2. She _____ very fast now.

3. They _____ slower than Felipe in the race yesterday.

4. The cat _____ after the mouse just before.

5. I _____ in all the races now.

GO ON TO THE NEXT PAGE

**41**

## THE VERBS *EAT, EATS, ATE,* AND *WILL EAT*

Fill in the blanks with **eat**, **eats**, **ate**, or **will eat**.

1. I _____ the best meal in the world yesterday.

2. My friends _____ too fast all the time.

3. _____ more slowly.

4. We _____ later.

5. The dog _____ us out of house and home soon.

## THE VERBS *TAKE, TAKES, TOOK,* AND *WILL TAKE*

Fill in the blanks with **take**, **takes**, **took**, or **will take**.

1. Please _____ that away.

2. I _____ her to the bus stop a moment ago.

3. They _____ us there later.

4. My parents _____ me out for my birthday tomorrow.

5. The test _____ two hours yesterday.

## THE VERBS *GROW, GROWS, GREW,* AND *WILL GROW*

Fill in the blanks with **grow**, **grows**, **grew**, or **will grow**.

1. My child _____ quite a bit last summer.

2. He _____ to be taller than his father soon.

3. My brother _____ a beard a month ago.

4. My money _____ too slowly now.

5. I _____ many things in my backyard now.

## ADVERBS (DESCRIBING WORDS)

Fill in each blank in the sentences with an adverb from this list. Use each adverb **once only**.

ADVERB LIST

down     here     soon     today     tomorrow

1. We will leave _____.

2. Those people live _____.

3. The child fell _____.

4. We will do that _____.

5. My brother got married _____.

GO ON TO THE NEXT PAGE

42

## ADVERBS (DESCRIBING WORDS)

Fill in each blank with an adverb that tells **how much**.

1. My dog runs _____ fast.

2. That man is _____ mean.

3. Do that _____ carefully.

4. Is that _____ hard for you?

5. He is _____ clever.

## THE WORDS *GOOD* AND *WELL*

Fill in each blank with either **good** or **well**.

1. I want _____ health for my family.

2. He was not feeling _____ yesterday.

3. That player runs _____.

4. The food smells _____.

5. She bakes cakes _____.

## SHOWING OWNERSHIP OR BELONGING TO (POSSESSION)

For each of the following nouns, write the plural noun and the noun that shows plural ownership.

| | PLURAL NOUN | PLURAL NOUN SHOWING OWNERSHIP |
|---|---|---|
| 1. wife | _____ | _____ |
| 2. foot | _____ | _____ |
| 3. safe | _____ | _____ |
| 4. pass | _____ | _____ |
| 5. match | _____ | _____ |
| 6. shelf | _____ | _____ |
| 7. baby | _____ | _____ |
| 8. child | _____ | _____ |
| 9. church | _____ | _____ |
| 10. car | _____ | _____ |

GO ON TO THE NEXT PAGE

## CONTRACTIONS (SHORTENING WORDS)

Write the contractions for the following words.

1. will not  _____
2. she has  _____
3. they are  _____
4. we will,  _____
5. I will  _____

6. I have  _____
7. cannot  _____
8. does not  _____
9. they will  _____
10. she is  _____

## COMMAS IN DATES AND ADDRESSES

Write the following over correctly. Add necessary commas.

1. may 21 1991  _____

2. theodore marcus  _____

   325 ford avenue  _____

   new york new york 10022  _____

3. august 3 1965  _____

4. september 10 1947  _____

5. linda roth  _____

   42 jefferson drive  _____

   philadelphia pennsylvania 19150  _____

## WRITING THE TIME OF DAY

Write each time in numbers with **A.M.** or **P.M.**

1. Half-past ten at night  _____
2. A quarter past eleven at night  _____
3. Ten past one in the morning  _____
4. Twenty-five past six in the evening  _____
5. Twenty past ten in the morning  _____

GO ON TO THE NEXT PAGE

## THE WORDS *A* AND *AN*

Put **a** or **an** before each of the following.

1. _____ used van

2. _____ huge tool

3. _____ hole

4. _____ water bottle

5. _____ answer

6. _____ uniform

7. _____ house

8. _____ year

9. _____ tray

10. _____ elephant

## WRITING AN INVITATION

Write a letter to invite someone to a party at your house.

## ADDRESSING AN ENVELOPE

Address this envelope to the person you are inviting to your party.

GO ON TO THE NEXT PAGE

## SPELLING

The following are misspelled words. Write them over correctly.

1. bussiness _____
2. alwys _____
3. fourty _____
4. prety _____
5. saturday _____
6. febuary _____
7. contry _____
8. yeserday _____
9. gues _____
10. anwer _____

11. alot _____
12. allready _____
13. freind _____
14. wedesday _____
15. wriet _____
16. wuman _____
17. soem _____
18. dokter _____
19. tusday _____
20. daer _____

## ALPHABETIZING (USING THE DICTIONARY)

Use the guide words **want** and **wash** to answer the questions. Write **Yes** or **No** in each blank.

1. Is the word **waste** on this page? _____
2. Is the word **was** on this page? _____
3. Is the word **war** on this page? _____
4. Is the word **warn** on this page? _____
5. Is the word **warm** on this page? _____

**STOP** CHECK ANSWERS BEGINNING ON PAGE 122.

Count how many items you answered correctly in each **Section** of the Review. Write your score per section in the **My Scores** column. If all your section scores are as high as the **Good Scores**, go on to the next stage of your study in *Power English*. If any of your section scores are lower than the **Good Scores**, study the lessons on the assigned **Review Pages** in *Power English 4* again before you go on.

| Section | Good Scores | My Scores | Review Pages |
|---|---|---|---|
| Capitalizing (Common Nouns and Proper Nouns) | 16–20 | | 2–3, 26, 54, 78, 102 |
| Singular and Plural Subjects | 8, 9, or 10 | | 5, 27, 55, 79 |
| Sentence Parts | 4 or 5 | | 6, 28 |
| Recognizing Sentences | 4 or 5 | | 7 |
| Word Order in Sentences | 2 | | 29 |
| End Marks | 4 or 5 | | 8 |
| Writing Sentences with Compound Subjects | 2 | | 30–31 |
| Combining Sentences | 4 or 5 | | 32–33, 104 |
| Combining Sentences | 4 or 5 | | 34–35, 56–57, 80–81 |
| Shortening Sentences with Commas | 4 or 5 | | 105, 106 |
| Adjectives (Describing Words) | 4 or 5 | | 9 |
| Adjectives (Describing Words) and Linking Words | 4 or 5 | | 58 |
| The Pronouns **I, You, He, She, It, We,** and **They** | 4 or 5 | | 36–37 |
| The Pronouns **Me, Him, Her, Us,** and **Them** | 4 or 5 | | 59, 85, 109 |

| Section | Good Scores | My Scores | Review Pages |
|---|---|---|---|
| More Than One (Noun Plurals) | 8, 9, or 10 | | 84 |
| Agreement of Subject and Verb | 4 or 5 | | 107, 108 |
| Verbs (Action Words): Present Time | 4 or 5 | | 10 |
| The Verbs **Run**, **Runs**, **Ran**, and **Will Run** | 4 or 5 | | 38, 39 |
| The Verbs **Eat**, **Eats**, **Ate**, and **Will Eat** | 4 or 5 | | 60, 61 |
| The Verbs **Take**, **Takes**, **Took**, and **Will Take** | 4 or 5 | | 86, 87 |
| The Verbs **Grow**, **Grows**, **Grew**, and **Will Grow** | 4 or 5 | | 110, 111 |
| Adverbs (Describing Words) | 4 or 5 | | 40–41 |
| Adverbs (Describing Words) | 4 or 5 | | 62 |
| The Words **Good** and **Well** | 4 or 5 | | 88, 112 |
| Showing Ownership or Belonging To (Possession) | 8, 9, or 10 | | 11, 12, 89, 113 |
| Contractions (Shortening Words) | 8, 9, or 10 | | 14, 63, 114 |
| Commas in Dates and Addresses | 4 or 5 | | 13 |
| Writing the Time of Day | 4 or 5 | | 42, 90 |
| The Words **A** and **An** | 8, 9, or 10 | | 64 |
| Writing an Invitation | A correct letter | | 65, 91 |
| Addressing an Envelope | Both addresses correct | | 66 |
| Spelling | 16–20 | | 15, 43, 67, 92, 115 |
| Alphabetizing (Using the Dictionary) | 4 or 5 | | 16, 44, 68, 93, 116 |

## CAPITALIZING

Write each of the following sentences over correctly.

1. my aunt barbara and uncle derrick live in the west and are moving east.

   _____

2. my cousin lives in west berlin and is coming to visit us in the united states of america.

   _____

   _____

3. my uncle charles fought in both world war II and the korean war.

   _____

4. her aunt monica is from italy and speaks italian, spanish, and french.

   _____

5. our chinese friend can speak english, russian, and chinese well.

   _____

## SINGULAR AND PLURAL SUBJECTS

Here is a list of nouns and pronouns from complete subjects. Write **S** in the blank if the subject is singular. Write **P** in the blank if the subject is plural.

1. Thomas and Drew _____    6. friends _____
2. She _____    7. They _____
3. We _____    8. women _____
4. wives _____    9. She and I _____
5. fathers _____    10. girl _____

GO ON TO THE NEXT PAGE

## SENTENCE PARTS

Find the words from Group Two, the predicate, that go with each complete subject from Group One. Write the letter in the blank.

GROUP ONE (COMPLETE SUBJECT)

____ 1. Stan Flemming

____ 2. His parents

____ 3. Christmas

____ 4. Often they

____ 5. His brothers and he

GROUP TWO (PREDICATE)

a. were both alcoholics.

b. was just another day.

c. have been on their own for years.

d. was used to hard times.

e. didn't even have a tree.

## END MARKS

Put the proper end mark at the end of each sentence.

1. Please show that to me

2. Is that all you want

3. How can you do these things

4. That is wonderful

5. Move

## AGREEMENT OF SUBJECT AND VERB

Underline the verb that is correct for the sentence.

1. The workers (**wants** or **want**) better hours.

2. Jim (**work** or **works**) six days every week.

3. His wife and children hardly (**sees** or **see**) him.

4. I (**needs** or **need**) more money to support my family.

5. It (**is** or **are**) hard with only one salary.

## COMBINING SENTENCES

Write one sentence that combines the sentences in each set.

1. My wife started work today.
   My wife likes her job.

   _____

2. Our children go to a friend's house.
   Our children stay there all day.

   _____

GO ON TO THE NEXT PAGE

**3.** My daughter plays outside in our friend's yard.
My son plays outside in our friend's yard.
My friend's son plays outside in our friend's yard.

_____

**4.** Our friend's yard has swings.
Our friend's yard has a sand box.
Our friend's yard has a jungle gym.

_____

**5.** My daughter likes it at our friend's house.
My son likes it at our friend's house.
My friend's son likes it at our friend's house.

_____

## SHORTENING SENTENCES

Write the following sentences over if they can be shortened by using commas. Write **C** in the blank below a sentence that cannot be shortened by using commas.

**1.** I earn a good living and enjoy life.

_____

**2.** Jamie and Al and Donald worry all the time.

_____

**3.** Jamie needs more money and needs more time and needs more work.

_____

**4.** Donald wants many things and doesn't want to work for them.

_____

**5.** Al complains a lot and his wife complains a lot and his son complains a lot.

_____

## PRONOUNS

Fill in each blank with the correct pronoun.

**1.** Please give _____ the book. (**I** or **me**)

**2.** She and _____ need more time. (**I** or **me**)

**3.** The dog bit _____. (**him** or **he**)

GO ON TO THE NEXT PAGE

4. Fabio likes _____ . (**she** or **her**)

5. The robber shot _____ . (**they** or **them**)

6. Lawrence told _____ the truth. (**we** or **us**)

7. That is not for _____ . (**she** or **her**)

8. This is between you and _____ . (**I** or **me**)

9. Are you against _____ ? (**we** or **us**)

10. The ball hit _____ . (**he** or **him**)

## PRONOUNS (SHOWING OWNERSHIP OR BELONGING TO)

In each blank in the sentences, write **mine**, **yours**, **his**, **hers**, **its**, **ours**, or **theirs**.

1. I own this coat.

   The coat is _____ .

2. He owns this book.

   The book is _____ .

3. The cat's tail is black

   _____ tail is black.

4. This is Anna's ring.

   The ring is _____ .

5. This is Mr. and Mrs. Neuman's house.

   This house is _____ .

## PRONOUNS AND WHAT THEY REFER TO

Fill in each blank with the correct pronoun.

1. The cat drinks milk.

   _____ drinks milk.

2. My brothers are in business together.

   _____ are in business together.

3. Peggy and I are here now.

   _____ are here now.

GO ON TO THE NEXT PAGE

52

**4.** Raul broke a tooth.

_____ broke a tooth.

**5.** Marta refuses to go out with him.

_____ refuses to go out with him.

**6.** The worker found _____ tool box.

**7.** The children ate _____ sandwiches.

**8.** Tina lost _____ wallet.

**9.** The dog wags _____ tail.

**10.** My brother owns _____ own house.

## ADJECTIVES

In each sentence, find the adjective that is used to compare. In the blank, write the comparing form of the adjective correctly. Add **more** or **most** or the **er** or **est** ending.

**1.** Larry is the stubborn person here.  _____

**2.** Carole is friendly than you.  _____

**3.** They look old than us.  _____

**4.** Kim is the charming person of all.  _____

**5.** This dog is quiet than yours.  _____

## ADJECTIVES AND LINKING VERBS

Fill in each blank in the sentences with an adjective from the list. Use each adjective **only once**.

ADJECTIVE LIST

fresher     nice     pretty     tired     unluckiest

**1.** Lauren looks as _____ as Ina.

**2.** Eric is the _____ man I have ever met.

**3.** I'll try to say something _____.

**4.** I am so _____ that my head aches.

**5.** The air smells _____ after a rain storm.

GO ON TO THE NEXT PAGE

## THE VERBS *BITE, BITES, BIT,* AND *WILL BITE*

Fill in each blank with **bite**, **bites**, **bit**, or **will bite**.

1. A dog _____ my child yesterday.

2. He _____ lots of people now.

3. Another dog _____ the mail carrier last week.

4. It _____ someone tomorrow again.

5. The dogs in my area _____ ten people last month.

## THE VERBS *GET, GETS, GOT,* AND *WILL GET*

Fill in each blank with **get**, **gets**, **got**, or **will get**.

1. This plant _____ lots of water now.

2. _____ that for me, please.

3. It _____ dark sooner now.

4. The days _____ longer soon.

5. I _____ a chill before.

## THE VERBS *BEGIN, BEGINS, BEGAN,* AND *WILL BEGIN*

Fill in each blank with **begin**, **begins**, **began**, or **will begin**.

1. The workers _____ fixing up my apartment soon.

2. The plumber _____ yesterday.

3. The work _____ at noon every day.

4. _____ that again, please.

5. I _____ my work earlier.

## THE VERBS *KNOW, KNOWS, KNEW,* AND *WILL KNOW*

Fill in each blank with **know**, **knows**, **knew**, or **will know**.

1. She _____ him very well now.

2. They _____ his name at the party last night.

3. Sam _____ everything soon.

4. I _____ more later on.

5. Aurora _____ it all yesterday.

GO ON TO THE NEXT PAGE

## THE VERBS *DRINK, DRINKS, DRANK,* AND *WILL DRINK*

Fill in each blank with **drink**, **drinks**, **drank**, or **will drink**.

1. _____ that more slowly.

2. She _____ too much now.

3. My kittens _____ their milk very fast soon.

4. I _____ to your health at the party tomorrow.

5. We _____ too much yesterday.

## ADVERBS

Write the adverb correctly in the blank in each sentence. Use the **er** or **est** ending.

1. Daniel runs _____ than you. (**fast**)

2. Helen and Barry danced _____ than Cathy and Bill. (**wild**)

3. Peter begins work _____ than Sanchez. (**late**)

4. You left the _____ of all the people. (**early**)

5. He drives the _____ of everyone. (**slow**)

## SHOWING OWNERSHIP OR BELONGING TO (POSSESSION)

Ten singular nouns follow. In the first blank, write the plural noun. In the second blank, write the noun that shows plural ownership.

| SINGULAR | PLURAL | PLURAL OWNERSHIP |
|---|---|---|
| 1. James | _____ | _____ |
| 2. dress | _____ | _____ |
| 3. child | _____ | _____ |
| 4. box | _____ | _____ |
| 5. mouse | _____ | _____ |
| 6. wife | _____ | _____ |
| 7. watch | _____ | _____ |
| 8. man | _____ | _____ |
| 9. lady | _____ | _____ |
| 10. house | _____ | _____ |

GO ON TO THE NEXT PAGE

## THE WORDS *ITS* AND *IT'S*

Fill in each blank with **its** or **it's**.

1. What is _____ name?

2. _____ a nice day today.

3. _____ food is getting cold.

4. They know _____ time to go.

5. Margaret said that _____ mother had three other kittens.

## THE WORDS *THEIR* AND *THEY'RE*

Fill in each blank with **their** or **they're**.

1. _____ parents are here now.

2. Where are _____ coats?

3. Did they say that _____ going?

4. _____ not here yet.

5. _____ car is stuck in the snow.

## THE WORDS *YOUR* AND *YOU'RE*

Fill in each blank with **your** or **you're**.

1. Is she _____ wife?

2. _____ very lucky.

3. What is _____ problem?

4. _____ sister just phoned.

5. We know _____ in trouble again.

## CONTRACTIONS

Write the contraction for each of the following.

1. I am _____

2. I will _____

3. he is _____

4. it has _____

5. she will _____

6. they are _____

7. it is _____

8. it will _____

9. they have _____

10. we have _____

GO ON TO THE NEXT PAGE

## THE WORDS *A* AND *AN*

Put **a** or **an** before each of the following.

1. _____ honest lady

2. _____ unused jar

3. _____ hour

4. _____ used car

5. _____ aunt

6. _____ early bird

7. _____ aide

8. _____ owner

9. _____ hen

10. _____ uncle

## WRITING AN INVITATION

On the lines below, write a letter to invite someone to a party at your house.

_____

_____

_____

_____

_____

_____

_____

_____

_____

_____

_____

_____

_____

GO ON TO THE NEXT PAGE

# WRITING A BUSINESS LETTER

Here are the parts of a business letter. The parts are not in order. Write the parts on the lines below so that they form a good business letter.

Sincerely yours,
Anthony Brown

532 Grant Avenue
Baltimore, Maryland 21231
May 11, 1990

Michael Rivera, President
ACE Lumber Company
411 Grover Road
Baltimore, Maryland 21229

Dear Mr. Rivera:

   I have been charged four times for material I have not received. Your billing department promised it would take care of the problem, but the bills keep coming. Please phone me as soon as possible so that we can straighten this out. My phone number is 555-9861.
   Thank you for your help.

GO ON TO THE NEXT PAGE

## ADDRESSING AN ENVELOPE

Fill out this envelope using the names and addresses of the persons in the business letter above.

_____

_____

_____


       _____

       _____

       _____

## SPELLING

The following words are spelled incorrectly. Spell them correctly.

1. prise _____
2. tonite _____
3. seperat _____
4. evry _____
5. belive _____
6. ofen _____
7. clohes _____
8. wher _____
9. tommorow _____
10. ninty _____

11. todey _____
12. janury _____
13. choos _____
14. eazy _____
15. suger _____
16. ninten _____
17. truely _____
18. techer _____
19. minut _____
20. truble _____

GO ON TO THE NEXT PAGE

## ALPHABETIZING (USING THE DICTIONARY)

Use the guide words **black** and **blare** to answer the questions. Write **Yes** or **No** in each blank.

1. Is the word **blame** on this page?  _____

2. Is the word **blast** on this page?  _____

3. Is the word **blade** on this page?  _____

4. Is the word **bland** on this page?  _____

5. Is the word **blaze** on this page?  _____

**STOP**  CHECK ANSWERS BEGINNING ON PAGE 124.

Count how many items you answered correctly in each **Section** of the Review. Write your score per section in the **My Scores** column. If all your section scores are as high as the **Good Scores**, go on to the next stage of your study in *Power English*. If any of your section scores are lower than the **Good Scores**, study the lessons on the assigned **Review Pages** in *Power English 5* again before you go on.

| Section | Good Scores | My Scores | Review Pages |
|---|---|---|---|
| Capitalizing | 4 or 5 | | 2, 26, 50, 76, 100 |
| Singular and Plural Subjects | 8, 9, or 10 | | 3, 27 |
| Sentence Parts | 4 or 5 | | 4 |
| End Marks | 4 or 5 | | 5 |
| Agreement of Subject and Verb | 4 or 5 | | 51, 77 |
| Combining Sentences | 4 or 5 | | 28, 52–53, 78–79, 102–103 |
| Shortening Sentences | 4 or 5 | | 29, 80, 104 |
| Pronouns | 8, 9, or 10 | | 6, 30, 54, 81, 105 |
| Pronouns (Showing Ownership or Belonging To) | 4 or 5 | | 55–56, 106 |
| Pronouns and What They Refer To | 8, 9, or 10 | | 82–83 |
| Adjectives | 4 or 5 | | 7, 57 |
| Adjectives and Linking Verbs | 4 or 5 | | 8 |
| The Verbs **Bite**, **Bites**, **Bit**, and **Will Bite** | 4 or 5 | | 9–10 |

| Section | Good Scores | My Scores | Review Pages |
|---|---|---|---|
| The Verbs **Get**, **Gets**, **Got**, and **Will Get** | 4 or 5 | | 32–33 |
| The Verbs **Begin**, **Begins**, **Began**, and **Will Begin** | 4 or 5 | | 58–59 |
| The Verbs **Know**, **Knows**, **Knew**, and **Will Know** | 4 or 5 | | 84–85 |
| The Verbs **Drink**, **Drinks**, **Drank**, and **Will Drink** | 4 or 5 | | 107–108 |
| Adverbs | 4 or 5 | | 34, 109 |
| Showing Ownership or Belonging To (Possession) | 8, 9, or 10 | | 35, 86 |
| The Words **Its** and **It's** | 4 or 5 | | 61 |
| The Words **Their** and **They're** | 4 or 5 | | 87 |
| The Words **Your** and **You're** | 4 or 5 | | 110 |
| Contractions | 8, 9, or 10 | | 11 |
| The Words **A** and **An** | 8, 9, or 10 | | 62 |
| Writing an Invitation | A correct letter | | 14–15 |
| Writing a Business Letter | A correct letter | | 36–37, 38–39, 63–64, 111–112 |
| Addressing an Envelope | Both addresses correct | | 88–89, 113 |
| Spelling | 16–20 | | 16, 40, 65, 90, 114 |
| Alphabetizing (Using the Dictionary) | 4 or 5 | | 17, 66, 91, 115 |

## CAPITALIZING

Correct the following nouns that are capitalized incorrectly. Put a **C** in the blank by those that are correct.

1. uncle _____
2. senator _____
3. moore computers _____
4. drake carpenters _____
5. disneyland _____

6. mother Theresa _____
7. aunt Margaret _____
8. plumber _____
9. parent _____
10. sears building _____

## SINGULAR AND PLURAL SUBJECTS

Underline the nouns and pronouns in the complete subject that control the verb in each of the following sentences. Write **S** in the blank if the subject of the sentence is singular. Write **P** in the blank if the subject of the sentence is plural.

1. My parents' apartment is on Main Street. _____
2. The girl and boy looked frightened and tired. _____
3. This sweater's buttons are all broken. _____
4. Emily's teeth need to be cleaned. _____
5. My wife's parents are visiting us now. _____

## AGREEMENT OF SUBJECT AND VERB

Underline the verb that is correct for each sentence.

1. My brother's wife (**have** or **has**) an excellent job.
2. The team's stars (**want** or **wants**) more money.
3. Her children's teachers (**is** or **are**) very nice.
4. Harry's business (**need** or **needs**) more help.
5. Mr. Garfield's brothers (**is** or **are**) in prison.

GO ON TO THE NEXT PAGE

## COMBINING SENTENCES

Write one sentence that combines all the sentences in each set.

1. José has his own used car.
   Peter has his own used car.
   Janet has her own used car.

   _____

   _____

2. Holly rents her own apartment today.
   Jeff rents his own apartment today.
   Sally rents her own apartment today.

   _____

   _____

3. Ruth loves her husband a lot.
   Pat loves her husband a lot.
   Kim loves her husband a lot.

   _____

   _____

4. Lisa does her job very well.
   Albert does his job very well.
   Sharon does her job very well.

   _____

   _____

5. My boss knows his drinking limits well.
   My friend knows his drinking limits well.
   I know my drinking limits well.

   _____

   _____

GO ON TO THE NEXT PAGE

## COMBINING SENTENCES

Write one sentence that combines the two in each of the following pairs. Use a comma with **or**, **but**, or **and** in the sentence you write.

1. We are looking for a new home.
   We can't find one we can afford.

   _____

2. We have to find one soon.
   Our furniture will be out in the street.

   _____

3. I don't want us to live in a shelter.
   Our parents have no room for us.

   _____

4. I look for a place every day.
   My wife does all she can.

   _____

5. Our children will stay with a friend.
   My wife and I will stay at the shelter.

   _____

## COMBINING SENTENCES

For each of the following combinations, write a sentence over if it is not correct. Write a **C** in the blank following sentence combinations that are correct.

1. The shelter is a dangerous place, people rob you there.

   _____

2. People go around half-dressed, and many children do not go to school.

   _____

3. It is depressing to be in a shelter, I hate it there.

   _____

4. The shelter is warm, and it keeps you from freezing to death.

   _____

5. Many poor people could once afford to rent, now they have to live in a shelter.

   _____

GO ON TO THE NEXT PAGE

## DIRECT QUOTATIONS

Write these direct quotations correctly.

1. My girlfriend asked are we getting married soon?

   _____

2. Rodrico said I need to go back to school.

   _____

3. Cheryl asked why are you going to do that?

   _____

4. Diane asked why should I wait for you?

   _____

5. The child said that man is running after me.

   _____

## DIRECT AND INDIRECT QUOTATIONS

The following sentences contain direct quotations. Write each sentence over so that it contains an indirect quotation.

1. She said, "I am very happy with my used car."

   _____

2. James said, "I enjoy my work."

   _____

3. The woman said, "This man just stole my bag."

   _____

4. Brian said, "Allison and Joy were arriving soon."

   _____

5. Charles said, "Mr. Williams is a nice man."

   _____

GO ON TO THE NEXT PAGE

## THE PRONOUNS *ANYBODY, ANYONE, EVERYBODY, EVERYONE, NOBODY, NO ONE, SOMEBODY,* AND *SOMEONE*

Underline the verb that is correct for the sentence.

1. Everybody (**know** or **knows**) all about this.

2. Anyone (**is** or **are**) welcome to try this.

3. Somebody (**has** or **have**) the things I need.

4. Someone (**is** or **are**) coming here soon.

5. Nobody (**want** or **wants**) to own one of these.

## PRONOUNS (SHOWING OWNERSHIP OR BELONGING TO)

Fill in each blank correctly with a pronoun that shows ownership.

1. This is my van.

   The van is _____ .

2. This is Laura's apartment.

   This is _____

   apartment.

3. Claude's life savings are all gone.

   _____ life savings are

   all gone.

4. These are the men's tools.

   These are _____ tools.

   These tools are _____ .

5. The dog's nose is cold.

   _____ nose is cold.

## PRONOUNS AND WHAT THEY REFER TO

Fill in each blank with the correct pronoun. The pronoun should refer to the subject of the sentence.

1. My cat washes _____ paws all the time.

2. The owners gave _____ cat some milk.

3. Mohammed hurt _____ hand earlier.

4. Teresa loves _____ boyfriend.

5. The sun spread _____ rays on the earth.

GO ON TO THE NEXT PAGE

## THE PRONOUNS *WHO, WHOM,* AND *WHOSE*

Fill in each blank with **who, whom,** or **whose.**

1. To _____ are you waving?

2. _____ scarf is this?

3. _____ saw you there last night?

4. About _____ are you speaking?

5. _____ did this to you?

## END MARKS (PUNCTUATION)

Put the proper end mark at the end of each sentence.

1. He asked whether he could see the ring

2. Benjamin asked all about you

3. That is terrible

4. Why are you doing this

5. I asked who was going to be at the party

## ADJECTIVES

Fill in each blank with the correct adjective.

1. She has _____ problems than you. (**many, more,** or **most**)

2. My husband has _____ friends. (**many, more,** or **most**)

3. This is the _____ day of my life. (**good, better,** or **best**)

4. Sachiko likes this _____ than that. (**good, better,** or **best**)

5. We have the _____ votes here. (**many, more,** or **most**)

## REGULAR AND IRREGULAR VERBS

In the blank, write the form of each verb that shows action in the past.

1. help _____     6. do _____

2. go _____     7. bite _____

3. know _____     8. run _____

4. dry _____     9. play _____

5. has _____     10. forget _____

GO ON TO THE NEXT PAGE

## THE VERBS *CATCH*, *CATCHES*, *CAUGHT*, AND *WILL CATCH*

Fill in each blank with **catch**, **catches**, **caught**, or **will catch**.

1. John _____ a bad cold last week.

2. We _____ lots of fish in the lake tomorrow.

3. My cat _____ lots of mice now.

4. _____ this.

5. This player _____ very well now.

## USING THE WORDS *HAS* AND *HAVE* WITH VERBS

Fill in each blank with the correct verb or verb phrase.

1. We _____ there many times over the years. (**went** or **have gone**)

2. Arturo _____ me often this year. (**helped** or **has helped**)

3. The police _____ the house yesterday. (**searched** or **have searched**)

4. Sonia _____ cards yesterday. (**played** or **has played**)

5. Terry _____ with his family for a while. (**worked** or **has worked**)

## ADDING *ING* TO VERBS WITH A HELPING VERB

In each blank, write the verb phrase that describes action that is going on right now.

1. I _____ all my work clothes here. (**buy**)

2. Edith _____ in the door this minute. (**come**)

3. They _____ at the wrong house. (**stop**)

4. We _____ the groceries away. (**put**)

5. Molly and I _____ to classes now. (**go**)

GO ON TO THE NEXT PAGE

## THE VERB *BE*

Fill in each blank with **am, is, are, was, were, will be, has been,** or **have been**.

1. I _____ at the bus station for hours.

2. They _____ not there earlier.

3. My parents _____ at the dinner tomorrow.

4. Tony and Marie _____ here now.

5. It _____ very hot last week.

## THE VERBS *FORGET, FORGETS, FORGOT, WILL FORGET,* AND *FORGOTTEN*

Fill in each blank with **forget, forgets, forgot, will forget,** or **forgotten**.

1. We _____ all about that earlier.

2. They _____ too many things the past few weeks.

3. Wayne _____ many things now.

4. I _____ about it yesterday.

5. Tony _____ his glasses later.

## ADVERBS

In each blank, write the comparing form of the adverb correctly.

1. Charles talks _____ of her than of you. (**proudly**)

2. The drunken man drove the _____ of anyone I have ever seen. (**carelessly**)

3. Leslie dresses the _____ of everybody. (**beautifully**)

4. Sam jumped out of the way of the car _____ than his buddy. (**quickly**)

5. They dance _____ than we do. (**terribly**)

## THE WORDS *WELL, BETTER,* AND *BEST*

Fill in each blank with the correct form of the word **well**.

1. She does _____ in whatever she does.

2. Ying sings _____ than Felix.

GO ON TO THE NEXT PAGE

70

**3.** The twins do the _____ in their own business.

**4.** Junko plays the guitar _____ than Mateo.

**5.** Antoine and Wing drive their trucks _____ .

## SHOWING OWNERSHIP OR BELONGING TO (POSSESSION)

For each of the following write the form that shows ownership.

**1.** dress _____

**2.** men _____

**3.** boxes _____

**4.** wolves _____

**5.** wife _____

**6.** Charles _____

**7.** children _____

**8.** boys _____

**9.** house _____

**10.** wives _____

## THE COMMA

Each of the following sentences has two adjectives. Add commas between adjectives where they are needed. If a sentence needs no comma, write **NC** in the blank.

**1.** This poor hardworking woman needs help. _____

**2.** My fancy new sweater is ripped. _____

**3.** Her little old dog wears a coat in the winter. _____

**4.** Drink this nice fresh milk. _____

**5.** I have a favorite black couch. _____

## CONTRACTIONS

There are two contractions in each of these sentences. Each of the contractions stands for two words. Write those two words in the blanks below the sentences.

**1.** I'm a good worker, but they've failed to notice it.

_____     _____

**2.** I won't be there, but she's going.

_____     _____

**3.** I've known that it's too late to try to help him.

_____     _____

GO ON TO THE NEXT PAGE

**4.** It'll be some time before she's lost enough weight.

_____  _____

**5.** They'll tell her we've gone away.

_____  _____

## THE WORDS _A_ AND _AN_

Put **a** or **an** before each of the following.

1. _____ healthy person

2. _____ ear

3. _____ holy man

4. _____ x-ray

5. _____ aisle

6. _____ ocean

7. _____ aunt

8. _____ deer

9. _____ answer

10. _____ usual thing

## WRITING AN INVITATION

Write a letter to invite a friend to an anniversary party.

GO ON TO THE NEXT PAGE

## WRITING A BUSINESS LETTER

Write a business letter to answer an ad for a bus driver. Write to **Mary Kelly, Windsor School District, 368 Brook Drive, Boston, Massachusetts 02115.**

GO ON TO THE NEXT PAGE

## SPELLING

The following words are spelled incorrectly. Spell them correctly.

1. pleze _____
2. loos _____
3. thankgiving _____
4. holidy _____
5. beggining _____
6. sentince _____
7. neice _____
8. finaly _____
9. writen _____
10. sincerly _____

11. kwiet _____
12. untill _____
13. favrite _____
14. turky _____
15. enugh _____
16. exellent _____
17. sience _____
18. vegtables _____
19. thursdy _____
20. marrage _____

## ALPHABETIZING (USING THE PHONE BOOK)

Use the guide names **Kirk** and **Kroll** to answer the questions. Write **Yes** or **No** in each blank.

1. Is the name **Ellen Krane** on this page? _____
2. Is the name **Lori Klein** on this page? _____
3. Is the name **Gary Kirsh** on this page? _____
4. Is the name **Jill Krums** on this page? _____
5. Is the name **Julian Krolmer** on this page? _____

**STOP** CHECK ANSWERS BEGINNING ON PAGE 126.

Count how many items you answered correctly in each **Section** of the Review. Write your score per section in the **My Scores** column. If all your section scores are as high as the **Good Scores**, go on to the next stage of your study in *Power English*. If any of your section scores are lower than the **Good Scores**, study the lessons on the assigned **Review Pages** in *Power English 6* again before you go on.

| Section | Good Scores | My Scores | Review Pages |
|---|---|---|---|
| Capitalizing | 8, 9, or 10 | | 2, 26, 50, 74, 100 |
| Singular and Plural Subjects | 4 or 5 | | 3, 51 |
| Agreement of Subject and Verb | 4 or 5 | | 27 |
| Combining Sentences | 4 or 5 | | 4–7, 28–29, 52–53, 101 |
| Combining Sentences | 4 or 5 | | 30–31, 75, 102 |
| Combining Sentences | 4 or 5 | | 54–55, 76–77, 103 |
| Direct Quotations | 4 or 5 | | 78–79, 104–105 |
| Direct and Indirect Quotations | 4 or 5 | | 80–81, 106 |
| The Pronouns **Anybody, Anyone, Everybody, Everyone, Nobody, No One, Somebody,** and **Someone** | 4 or 5 | | 32, 56 |
| Pronouns (Showing Ownership or Belonging To) | 4 or 5 | | 33–34 |
| Pronouns and What They Refer To | 4 or 5 | | 9 |
| The Pronouns **Who, Whom,** and **Whose** | 4 or 5 | | 82, 108 |

| Section | Good Scores | My Scores | Review Pages |
|---|---|---|---|
| End Marks (Punctuation) | 4 or 5 | | 8, 107 |
| Adjectives | 4 or 5 | | 10 |
| Regular and Irregular Verbs | 8, 9, or 10 | | 11, 35 |
| The Verbs **Catch**, **Catches**, **Caught**, and **Will Catch** | 4 or 5 | | 57 |
| Using the Words **Has** and **Have** with Verbs | 4 or 5 | | 58–61, 83, 109 |
| Adding **ing** to Verbs with a Helping Verb | 4 or 5 | | 62, 84, 110 |
| The Verb **Be** | 4 or 5 | | 63, 111 |
| The Verbs **Forget**, **Forgets**, **Forgot**, **Will Forget**, and **Forgotten** | 4 or 5 | | 112 |
| Adverbs | 4 or 5 | | 12–13, 85 |
| The Words **Well**, **Better**, and **Best** | 4 or 5 | | 36 |
| Showing Ownership or Belonging To (Possession) | 8, 9, or 10 | | 14, 37 |
| The Comma | 4 or 5 | | 86 |
| Contractions | 4 or 5 | | 64 |
| The Words **A** and **An** | 8, 9, or 10 | | 87 |
| Writing an Invitation | A correct letter | | 15–16 |
| Writing a Business Letter | A correct letter | | 38–39, 88 |
| Spelling | 16–20 | | 17, 40, 65, 89, 113 |
| Alphabetizing (Using the Phone Book) | 4 or 5 | | 41, 66 |

## CAPITALIZING

Here is a list of nouns. Correct any nouns that are not written correctly. Put a **C** in the blank by those that are correct.

1. boulevard _____
2. holiday _____
3. west Berlin _____
4. History _____
5. Autumn _____

6. Senator _____
7. Season _____
8. uncle Joe _____
9. Company _____
10. chinese _____

## SINGULAR AND PLURAL SUBJECTS

Underline the nouns and pronouns in the complete subject that control the verb in each of the following sentences. Write **S** in the blank if the subject of the sentence is singular. Write **P** in the blank if the subject of the sentence is plural.

1. His father's sisters are nice. _____
2. Nobody is home today. _____
3. The children's dog is not well. _____
4. Everybody was here yesterday. _____
5. Someone needs that now. _____

## RECOGNIZING SENTENCES

Put a check (✓) by each of the sentences.

☐ 1. Wherever he goes.

☐ 2. After the play is over.

☐ 3. Stop.

☐ 4. My friend is not here.

☐ 5. When I can make it.

GO ON TO THE NEXT PAGE

## WORD ORDER IN SENTENCES

Use the following groups of words to write sentences. Add necessary commas.

1. Together José went Karen Ben Ann and business I into.

   _____

2. Customers shop we clean cook babysit for would we our and.

   _____

3. Until everything well we arguing money went began over.

   _____

4. Men paid felt the more they should women that than the get.

   _____

5. Said equal for equal I we that all work should pay get.

   _____

## COMBINING SENTENCES

Write one sentence that combines the two in each of the following pairs. Use a comma with **or**, **but**, or **and** in the sentence you write.

1. Jim's friend is a drug addict.
   Jim is not.

   _____

   _____

2. They have been friends since kindergarten.
   Jim cannot put up with his friend's drug problem.

   _____

   _____

3. Jim's friend must give up drugs.
   Jim will no longer be his friend.

   _____

   _____

4. Jim's friend uses other drug addicts' needles.
   They use his needle.

   _____

   _____

GO ON TO THE NEXT PAGE

**5.** Drug addicts think it's a sign of friendship to share needles. Jim thinks it's a death wish.

_____

_____

## SHORTENING SENTENCES

Shorten the following sentences by using commas.

**1.** My sister Sharon and my sister Carol and my sister Jennifer are visiting me tomorrow.

_____

_____

**2.** My pal Fred is nice and my pal Jay is nice and my pal Sean is nice.

_____

_____

**3.** Lynn put on her new coat and her new gloves and her new hat.

_____

_____

**4.** The train is late today and the bus is late today and the van is late today.

_____

_____

**5.** The man was injured on the bus earlier and the woman was injured on the bus earlier and the child was injured on the bus earlier.

_____

_____

## SENTENCE PARTS

Here are some sentence parts and some sentences. Underline each of the sentence parts. Put a check (√) by each of the sentences.

☐ **1.** After I buy something good.

☐ **2.** The men refused to go.

☐ **3.** Help.

☐ **4.** When they told us the truth.

☐ **5.** Stop that.

GO ON TO THE NEXT PAGE

## SENTENCE PARTS (DEPENDENT AND INDEPENDENT WORD GROUPS)

Find the dependent word group in each of the following sentences and underline it.

1. She became my best friend after she got out of jail.

2. She made a mistake when she was very young.

3. If people would let her forget, she could begin again.

4. Unless she gets a decent job, she will not make it.

5. She learned many things while she was in prison.

## DIRECT QUOTATIONS

Write these direct quotations correctly. Add the correct end mark.

1. Josh asked why won't people help her

_____

2. Sandy said it's because people do not trust her

_____

3. Rodrico asked what will happen to her

_____

4. Ann asked why do people have to be so mean

_____

5. Peter said many people have been hurt by being too trusting

_____

## DIRECT AND INDIRECT QUOTATIONS

The following sentences contain indirect quotations. Write each sentence over so that it contains a direct quotation.

1. Florence said that she is very happy to have such a nice family.

_____

2. Bill said that he needs another good rating from his boss.

_____

3. Betty said that this is one of the best things she has ever done.

_____

GO ON TO THE NEXT PAGE

**4.** Andrew said that he needs all the help he can get.

_____

**5.** Franco said that he never worked so hard in all his life.

_____

## END MARKS (PUNCTUATION MARKS)
Put the proper end mark at the end of each sentence.

1. Barbara asked where they were going

2. Larry said that he needed another job

3. What happened to your old job

4. He said that he and his boss had a fight

5. Eleni asked how you could get into a fight with your boss

## PRONOUNS
Fill in each blank with the correct pronoun.

1. Hiromu and _____ know _____ . (**them** and **I**)

2. _____ saw _____ . (**her** and **he**)

3. _____ know _____ . (**we** and **them**)

4. _____ like _____ . (**us** and **they**)

5. _____ slapped _____ . (**him** and **she**)

## PRONOUNS AND WHAT THEY REFER TO
Fill in each blank with the correct pronoun.

1. David sent _____ girlfriend a dozen roses.

2. The dog wagged _____ tail.

3. My friends love _____ new apartment.

4. I like _____ new job.

5. We need _____ rest.

GO ON TO THE NEXT PAGE

## PRONOUNS (SHOWING OWNERSHIP OR BELONGING TO)

Fill in each blank with a pronoun that shows ownership.

1. This is my cat.

   This cat is _____.

2. This is the Smiths' car.

   This car is _____.

3. This is my cat's bowl.

   This is _____ bowl.

4. This is Julio's business.

   This business is _____.

5. These are Laura's children.

   These children are _____.

## THE PRONOUNS *ANYBODY, ANYONE, EVERYBODY, EVERYONE, NOBODY, NO ONE, SOMEBODY,* AND *SOMEONE*

Underline the verb that is correct for the sentence.

1. Nobody (**want** or **wants**) to help him now.

2. Everybody (**was** or **were**) at the bowling alley last night.

3. Someone (**is** or **are**) not telling the truth.

4. Nobody (**know** or **knows**) us here.

5. Everyone (**has** or **have**) at least one of these.

## THE WORDS *WHO, WHOM,* AND *WHOSE*

Fill in each blank with **who, whom,** or **whose**.

1. _____ is going to tell her boss the truth?

2. Against _____ are you playing?

3. _____ sister are you dating?

4. _____ told you that about her?

5. To _____ will you give those flowers?

GO ON TO THE NEXT PAGE

# MORE THAN ONE (PLURAL)

Write the plural form of each of the following nouns.

1. wife _____
2. child _____
3. policeman _____
4. deer _____
5. foot _____

6. leaf _____
7. box _____
8. sheep _____
9. mouse _____
10. tooth _____

# ADJECTIVES AND LINKING VERBS

Fill in each blank in the sentences with an adjective from the list.

ADJECTIVE LIST

better    brightest    delicious    handsome    happier

1. The sun looks the _____ in the morning.

2. The air smells _____ after it rains than before.

3. Carol's dinners always taste very _____ .

4. Irene sounds _____ than she really is.

5. Alejandro looks _____ today.

# REGULAR AND IRREGULAR VERBS

Write two forms for each verb: the form for past, and the form for up to now (with **has**).

| REGULAR VERBS | | | | IRREGULAR VERBS | | |
|---|---|---|---|---|---|---|
| | PAST | UP TO NOW | | | PAST | UP TO NOW |
| 1. change | _____ | _____ | | 6. go | _____ | _____ |
| 2. call | _____ | _____ | | 7. steal | _____ | _____ |
| 3. answer | _____ | _____ | | 8. write | _____ | _____ |
| 4. talk | _____ | _____ | | 9. lie | _____ | _____ |
| 5. work | _____ | _____ | | 10. speak | _____ | _____ |

GO ON TO THE NEXT PAGE

## THE VERB *BE*

Fill in each blank with the correct form of the verb **be**.

1. Kim and Herb _____ at the party tomorrow.

2. I _____ not at home yesterday.

3. Nobody _____ here all week.

4. Everybody _____ at your party last night.

5. Donna _____ a very happy person now.

## THE VERBS *SPEAK, SPEAKS, SPOKE, WILL SPEAK, HAS SPOKEN, HAVE SPOKEN,* AND *HAD SPOKEN*

Fill in each blank with the correct form of the verb **speak**.

1. We _____ to him tomorrow about it.

2. Our teacher _____ to us before.

3. Celia had _____ to the police already.

4. Sadahiro and I have _____ to them a few times.

5. My parrot _____ a lot now.

## THE VERBS *STEAL, STEALS, STOLE, WILL STEAL, HAS STOLEN, HAVE STOLEN,* AND *HAD STOLEN*

Fill in each blank with the correct form of the verb **steal**.

1. David has _____ many things from the department store.

2. The police caught the man who had _____ the car.

3. Rita said she _____ a dress tomorrow.

4. She _____ a coat last week from a different store.

5. People have _____ from Julio's store.

## THE VERBS *WRITE, WRITES, WROTE, WILL WRITE, HAS WRITTEN,* AND *HAVE WRITTEN,* AND *HAD WRITTEN*

Fill in each blank with the correct form of the verb **write**.

1. I have _____ to them many times.

2. Carla _____ me a letter last week.

3. Tina _____ a note to her later today.

4. Andres _____ letters to his grandparents now.

5. Tara _____ good stories yesterday.

GO ON TO THE NEXT PAGE

## THE VERBS *LAY, LAYS, LAID, WILL LAY, HAS LAID, HAVE LAID,* AND *HAD LAID*

Fill in each blank with the correct form of the verb **lay**.

1. George _____ his wallet on the table yesterday.

2. He has _____ it there every day this week.

3. The goose _____ eggs.

4. I _____ my packages on the kitchen table later.

5. _____ those things here.

## THE VERBS *LIE, LIES, LAY, WILL LIE, HAS LAIN, HAVE LAIN,* AND *HAD LAIN*

Fill in each blank with the correct form of the verb **lie**.

1. Mary has _____ in bed all day today.

2. Jeff _____ in bed yesterday when he was ill.

3. This dog _____ very quietly when it sleeps.

4. The poor man has _____ in the road for hours.

5. During the war, the soldiers had _____ in ditches for days.

## THE VERBS *TEACH* AND *LEARN*

Fill in each blank with the correct form of **teach** or **learn**.

1. My father _____ me many things when he was alive.

2. I also _____ many things from my mother when I was a child.

3. Scott _____ many things from his parents now.

4. When we have children, we _____ them to be good and honest.

5. The prisoner said he had _____ his lesson.

## ADVERBS

In each blank, write the comparing form of the adverb correctly.

1. Roger is doing _____ now than before. (**bad**)

2. That man works the _____ of anyone I know. (**well**)

3. I have worked the _____ I ever have. (**hard**)

4. She acted even _____ at this party than at the last one. (**silly**)

5. We have to jump _____ each time. (**high**)

GO ON TO THE NEXT PAGE

## SHOWING OWNERSHIP OR BELONGING TO (POSSESSION)

The nouns that show ownership in these sentences are written incorrectly. Find each of those nouns and write its correct form in the blank that follows.

1. Our childrens' coats are missing. _____

2. The deers' ear was hurt. _____

3. Mr. Jones' apartment is too cold. _____

4. The churchs' door was broken in the storm. _____

5. My wifes' parents are visiting us tomorrow. _____

## THE WORDS *ITS* AND *IT'S*, *THEIR* AND *THEY'RE*, AND *WHOSE* AND *WHO'S*

Fill in each blank with the correct word.

1. _____ name is on this card? (**Who's** or **Whose**)

2. Why is _____ food still here? (**it's** or **its**)

3. I know _____ too late to go now. (**it's** or **its**)

4. _____ been on the trip? (**Who's** or **Whose**)

5. _____ not here now. (**Their** or **They're**)

## THE COMMA

Add commas in the following sentences if they are needed. If a sentence needs no comma, write **NC** in the blank following the sentence.

1. Indeed that is a cute little black kitten. _____

2. The big fat cat however is angry. _____

3. For example the large mean dog growled and jumped at us. _____

4. A tall young man stopped to help us. _____

5. Of course we were very grateful. _____

## ABBREVIATIONS (SHORTENED WORDS)

Fill in each blank with the correct abbreviation.

1. _____ Garcia lives on Grand _____. (**doctor; avenue**)

2. We visited _____ Peter Bartlett who lives on Ford _____.

   (**reverend; street**)

GO ON TO THE NEXT PAGE

3. _____ Collins visited the Grossman _____ on Taylor

_____ . (**doctor; company; road**)

4. _____ Alan Gates will meet us on Southern _____ at

10:00 _____ . (**reverend; boulevard; before noon**)

5. _____ Huang and I have a date at 1:30 _____ .

(**doctor; after noon**)

## CONTRACTIONS

Write the contractions for the following words.

1. we have _____   6. he has _____

2. I am _____   7. should not _____

3. they will _____   8. I will _____

4. she is _____   9. will not _____

5. cannot _____   10. do not _____

## WRITING THE TIME OF DAY

Write the following times correctly.

1. 1235 am _____   6. 705 pm _____

2. 445 pm _____   7. 1105 am _____

3. 1025 pm _____   8. 625 am _____

4. 910 pm _____   9. 730 am _____

5. 630 am _____   10. 230 pm _____

## THE WORDS *A* AND *AN*

Put **a** or **an** before each of the following.

1. _____ orphan   6. _____ honor

2. _____ orange   7. _____ apartment

3. _____ error   8. _____ hole

4. _____ van   9. _____ honest mistake

5. _____ pretty girl   10. _____ foolish person

GO ON TO THE NEXT PAGE

## WRITING PARAGRAPHS

Underline the words that help link the sentences in the following paragraph.

Last year was not the best year of our lives. First, my husband lost his job. Then he became very ill. Eventually, we lost all our money trying to save him, and I had to give up my job to take care of him. Finally, the worst blow of all came when we were put out of our apartment, and we had to go on welfare.

## ORGANIZING SENTENCES INTO A PARAGRAPH

Write the following sentences over in a paragraph that makes sense. First, write the introductory sentence. Then add the other sentences in an order that is logical.

Later he was allowed to turn down a certain assignment because it would have meant leaving Mia behind. Thanks to the army, they were going to be separated for the first time in their married lives. Moreover, he was uncomfortable about being separated from his wife for several months. Nate and Mia felt miserable on their way to the train station. As a result, Nate was angry that the army did not keep its promise. Finally, however, he got orders to take the assignment he had turned down. At first the army had told Nate that he would never be given a peacetime assignment that would separate him from his wife.

_____

_____

_____

_____

_____

_____

_____

_____

_____

GO ON TO THE NEXT PAGE

## SENTENCE VARIETY

Write the following paragraph over to make it more pleasing to read.

My father is a hard worker. My mother is a hard worker. My sister is a hard worker. I am a hard worker. Our family was on welfare. That was when my sister and I were young. Our parents wanted to get off welfare. They each found two jobs. They each worked on two jobs. They encouraged my sister and me to work as soon as we were old enough. They encouraged us to save money. My sister and I continue to work hard. We follow our parents' example.

_____

_____

_____

_____

_____

_____

_____

## PROOFREADING

Write the following paragraph over correctly.

Stuart is the oldst child in his famly. he is hardly out of his Teens but he have been workin for a number of Year to help out his Family. he have had many jobs, he has never let anyone down. now he is in college and suportin hisself. his Family is very proud of Him.

_____

_____

_____

_____

_____

_____

_____

GO ON TO THE NEXT PAGE

## WRITING AN INVITATION

Write a letter to invite someone to a bridal shower or a bachelor party.

_____

_____

_____

_____

_____

_____

_____

_____

_____

_____

_____

_____

_____

GO ON TO THE NEXT PAGE

# WRITING A BUSINESS LETTER

You ordered some gloves. Write a letter to complain that you received the wrong pair. The gloves were advertised in the Daily News. You do not know the name of the president of the department store. Write to the **president, Harper's Department Store, 156 Broadway**, New York, New York 10003.

## SPELLING

Spell the following words correctly.

1. onlie _____
2. cuosin _____
3. aggain _____
4. coler _____
5. becuz _____
6. sinse _____
7. somtimes _____
8. helth _____
9. develope _____
10. insted _____

11. naim _____
12. picknick _____
13. goodbuy _____
14. cugh _____
15. recieve _____
16. shoos _____
17. ake _____
18. straght _____
19. jugement _____
20. jist _____

## ALPHABETIZING (USING THE PHONE BOOK)

Use the guide names **Brant** and **Bravern** to answer the questions. Write **Yes** or **No** in each blank.

1. Is the name **Harry Brazer** on this page? _____
2. Is the name **Judith Braile** on this page? _____
3. Is the name **Carol Brano** on this page? _____
4. Is the name **Robert Bratter** on this page? _____
5. Is the name **Harold Braso** on this page? _____

STOP CHECK ANSWERS BEGINNING ON PAGE 128.

Count how many items you answered correctly in each **Section** of the Review. Write your score per section in the **My Scores** column. If all your section scores are as high as the **Good Scores**, go on to the next stage of your study in *Power English*. If any of your section scores are lower than the **Good Scores**, study the lessons on the assigned **Review Pages** in *Power English 7* again before you go on.

| Section | Good Scores | My Scores | Review Pages |
|---|---|---|---|
| Capitalizing | 8, 9, or 10 | | 2–3, 26, 48, 72–73, 96–97 |
| Singular and Plural Subjects | 4 or 5 | | 4 |
| Recognizing Sentences | 4 or 5 | | 5 |
| Word Order in Sentences | 4 or 5 | | 98 |
| Combining Sentences | 4 or 5 | | 7, 27, 49–52, 74–75 |
| Shortening Sentences | 4 or 5 | | 28 |
| Sentence Parts | 4 or 5 | | 6, 29 |
| Sentence Parts (Dependent and Independent Word Groups) | 4 or 5 | | 30, 53, 76 |
| Direct Quotations | 4 or 5 | | 8, 31 |
| Direct and Indirect Quotations | 4 or 5 | | 32–33 |
| End Marks (Punctuation Marks) | 4 or 5 | | 9, 77 |
| Pronouns | 4 or 5 | | 34 |
| Pronouns and What They Refer To | 4 or 5 | | 99 |
| Pronouns (Showing Ownership or Belonging To) | 4 or 5 | | 78–79 |
| The Pronouns **Anybody, Anyone, Everybody, Everyone, Nobody, No One, Somebody,** and **Someone** | 4 or 5 | | 55 |
| The Words **Who, Whom,** and **Whose** | 4 or 5 | | 80 |

| Section | Good Scores | My Scores | Review Pages |
|---|---|---|---|
| More Than One (Plural) | 8, 9, or 10 | | 35 |
| Adjectives and Linking Verbs | 4 or 5 | | 10 |
| Regular and Irregular Verbs | 8, 9, or 10 | | 11 |
| The Verb **Be** | 4 or 5 | | 12 |
| The Verbs **Speak, Speaks, Spoke, Will Speak, Has Spoken, Have Spoken**, and **Had Spoken** | 4 or 5 | | 13 |
| The Verbs **Steal, Steals, Stole, Will Steal, Has Stolen, Have Stolen**, and **Had Stolen** | 4 or 5 | | 36 |
| The Verbs **Write, Writes, Wrote, Will Write, Has Written, Have Written**, and **Had Written** | 4 or 5 | | 56 |
| The Verbs **Lay, Lays, Laid, Will Lay, Has Laid, Have Laid**, and **Had Laid** | 4 or 5 | | 81 |
| The Verbs **Lie, Lies, Lay, Will Lie, Has Lain, Have Lain**, and **Had Lain** | 4 or 5 | | 100 |
| The Verbs **Teach** and **Learn** | 4 or 5 | | 101 |
| Adverbs | 4 or 5 | | 37 |
| Showing Ownership or Belonging To (Possession) | 4 or 5 | | 38, 57 |
| The Words **Its** and **It's, Their** and **They're**, and **Whose** and **Who's** | 4 or 5 | | 102 |
| The Comma | 4 or 5 | | 58, 103 |
| Abbreviations (Shortened Words) | 4 or 5 | | 59 |
| Contractions | 8, 9, or 10 | | 39 |
| Writing the Time of Day | 8, 9, or 10 | | 83 |
| The Words **A** and **An** | 8, 9, or 10 | | 14 |
| Writing Paragraphs | 4 | | 84 |

| Section | Good Scores | My Scores | Review Pages |
|---|---|---|---|
| Organizing Sentences into a Paragraph | 7 | | 85–86, 104–105 |
| Sentence Variety | A correct paragraph | | 106–107 |
| Proofreading | 15–18 | | 87, 108 |
| Writing an Invitation | A correct letter | | 15–16 |
| Writing a Business Letter | A correct letter | | 60–61 |
| Spelling | 16–20 | | 17, 40, 62, 88, 109 |
| Alphabetizing (Using the Phone Book) | 4 or 5 | | 63, 110 |

## CAPITALIZING

Write each sentence over correctly. Include the proper punctuation for each sentence.

1. bill said i am visiting my mother at 6:30 pm

_____

2. marianne asked does she live near us on sherry rd

_____

3. nicole asked whether we were meeting later at the perry co

_____

4. eric said i am going north soon to meet my friends at their house on dover ave

_____

5. dr nettleton and rev henry are meeting at 9:30 am

_____

## SINGULAR AND PLURAL SUBJECTS

Underline the nouns and pronouns in the complete subject that control the verb in each of the following sentences. Write **S** in the blank if the subject of the sentence is singular. Write **P** in the blank if the subject of the sentence is plural.

1. Everybody is coming to Frank's party.          _____

2. The Davises' neighbors are from Puerto Rico.          _____

3. My brother's used car refuses to run.          _____

4. Nobody was present at the meeting yesterday.          _____

5. Tim and I are getting married soon.          _____

## RECOGNIZING SENTENCES

Put a check (√) by each of the sentences.

☐ 1. After all the problems and fights.

☐ 2. No one can live here.

☐ 3. Whether they can stay or not.

☐ 4. Where did you say you went?

☐ 5. What we want.

GO ON TO THE NEXT PAGE

## WORD ORDER IN SENTENCES

Use the following groups of words to write sentences. Include necessary commas.

1. On school Sally Fred starting Carmela I again Monday are and.

_____

2. English courses mathematics history computers we taking and in are.

_____

3. Jobs we order need to skills find in gain to some.

_____

4. Secretary to a I school because going I am to want become.

_____

5. Read speak secretary well a needs be to write and able to.

_____

## COMBINING SENTENCES

Write one sentence that combines the two in each of the following pairs. Use a comma with **or**, **but**, or **and** in the sentences you write.

1. Patience is very important.
   Sometimes it is hard to be patient.

_____

2. Some people have a lot.
   They are never satisfied.

_____

3. Some people have very little.
   They have nothing to look forward to.

_____

4. Life can be a great adventure.
   It can be a nightmare.

_____

5. Approach life with a positive attitude.
   It will wear you down.

_____

GO ON TO THE NEXT PAGE

## SHORTENING SENTENCES

Shorten the following sentences using commas.

1. Raimundo is my good friend and Daniella is my good friend and Hossein is my good friend.

   _____

   _____

2. Romain likes his coffee hot and Yuriko likes her coffee hot and Paolo likes his coffee hot.

   _____

   _____

3. I will meet Rosa later and I will meet King later and I will meet Tran later.

   _____

   _____

4. Gordon is very excited and Robin is very excited and Monique is very excited.

   _____

   _____

5. Donna has a nice apartment and Alma has a nice apartment and Akemi has a nice apartment.

   _____

   _____

## SENTENCE PARTS (DEPENDENT AND INDEPENDENT WORD GROUPS)

Underline the dependent word group in each of the following sentences.

1. Many drop-out students are going back to school because they want to get better jobs.

2. Hugo dropped out of school when he was sixteen years old.

3. He has drifted from one job to another because he is not happy.

4. Until he learns to read, write, and speak better, he will have difficulty getting a good job.

5. Hugo can turn his life around if he really wants to do so.

GO ON TO THE NEXT PAGE

## COMBINING INDEPENDENT AND DEPENDENT WORD GROUPS

Combine the two sentences in each of the following pairs. Use one of the linking words from the list. Add necessary commas. Use a linking word **once only**.

LINKING WORDS

after    as    because    unless    when

1. The terrorist boarded the plane.
   He had a gun.

   _____

   _____

2. The terrorist pointed the gun at people.
   He walked up and down the aisle.

   _____

   _____

3. The passengers were very frightened.
   The terrorist looked crazy.

   _____

   _____

4. The terrorist would kill the passengers.
   The pilot flew him to his homeland.

   _____

   _____

5. The terrorist shot a passenger.
   The pilot jumped out of his seat and disarmed him.

   _____

   _____

## DIRECT QUOTATIONS

Write these direct quotations correctly. Put in the correct end marks.

1. Cleo said that is really a very good idea

   _____

2. Howard asked why are you always so late

   _____

GO ON TO THE NEXT PAGE

3. Orlando asked is it wise to do this now

_____

4. Ellen said it seemed fine to me

_____

5. Fung asked did you finish the job yet

_____

## DIRECT AND INDIRECT QUOTATIONS

The following sentences contain indirect quotations. Write each sentence over so that it contains a direct quotation.

1. Judy said that she wants to help the poor.

_____

2. Florence said that her brothers are fine gentlemen.

_____

3. Mrs. Adams said that her son needs help.

_____

4. Mr. O'Connell said that he likes the people at work.

_____

5. Mrs. Ramirez said that her husband is doing well.

_____

## END MARKS (PUNCTUATION MARKS)

Put the proper end mark at the end of each sentence.

1. Robert asked why we are not going tonight

2. The twins are doing well now

3. Is that really your house

4. Why are you being so mean

5. Elias asked whether he could attend the meeting

GO ON TO THE NEXT PAGE

## PRONOUNS AND WHAT THEY REFER TO

Fill in each blank with the correct pronoun.

1. Somebody hurt _____ foot at work.

2. The baritone got back _____ voice.

3. The rose lost _____ color.

4. The carpenters want _____ back pay.

5. I need _____ coffee in the morning.

## PRONOUNS (SHOWING OWNERSHIP OR BELONGING TO)

In each blank in the sentences, write a pronoun that shows ownership.

1. There is her hat.

   The hat is _____ .

2. Here are the Smiths' coats.

   These coats are _____ .

3. The bird's wing is hurt.

   _____ wing is hurt.

4. The birds' nest just fell.

   _____ nest just fell.

5. My boyfriend's smile is nice.

   _____ smile is nice.

## THE WORDS *EACH, EITHER . . . OR,* AND *NEITHER . . . NOR*

Underline the correct verb.

1. Each boy and girl (**has** or **have**) a book.

2. Each window in the room (**is** or **are**) open.

3. Neither my friend nor my enemies (**is** or **are**) here.

4. Either he or Jim (**has** or **have**) to go there.

5. Neither my brothers nor my father (**knows** or **know**) her.

GO ON TO THE NEXT PAGE

## ADJECTIVES AND ADVERBS

Fill in each blank with the correct adjective or adverb.

1. A _____ child screamed _____.

   (**youngest, young, loudly**)

2. My _____ friend runs _____ than you. (**best, fast, faster**)

3. Janet's _____ brother left _____.

   (**taller, quicker, quickly**)

4. The _____ man of all works _____. (**older, oldest, here**)

5. The _____ house burned _____.

   (**old, complete, completely**)

## REGULAR AND IRREGULAR VERBS

Write three forms for each verb: the form for past, the form for up to now (with **has**), and the form for right now (with **is**).

| | PAST | UP TO NOW | RIGHT NOW |
|---|---|---|---|
| **1.** learn | _____ | _____ | _____ |
| **2.** cry | _____ | _____ | _____ |
| **3.** cut | _____ | _____ | _____ |
| **4.** speak | _____ | _____ | _____ |
| **5.** write | _____ | _____ | _____ |

## USING THE WORDS *HAS* AND *HAVE* WITH VERBS

Fill in each blank with the correct verb or verb phrase.

1. The police _____ them out of business hundreds of times. (**put** or

   **have put**)

2. Everybody _____ the drug dealers will be back soon. (**bets** or **has bet**)

3. The drugs _____ a fortune, but people still buy them. (**have cost** or

   **cost**)

4. We _____ many times on this. (**have bet** or **bet**)

5. We _____ that there yesterday. (**have put** or **put**)

GO ON TO THE NEXT PAGE

## THE VERBS *CUT, CUTS, WILL CUT, HAS CUT, HAVE CUT,* AND *HAD CUT*

Fill in each blank with the proper form of the verb **cut**.

1. I _____ my finger earlier.

2. Her father _____ the roast later.

3. The players _____ themselves on the ice often before.

4. Jack and Herbert _____ the birthday cake soon.

5. Fernando _____ school too many times.

## THE VERBS *SET* AND *SIT*

Fill in each blank with the proper form of **sit** or **set**.

1. Dora _____ the table earlier.

2. _____ down in this chair.

3. They _____ the gifts under the tree soon.

4. What did you _____ on top of my papers?

5. Jill _____ too close to the baby before.

## THE WORDS *CAN* AND *MAY*

Fill in each blank with **can** or **may**.

1. She _____ run faster than you.

2. _____ I borrow this dish?

3. _____ you do this work?

4. Dan _____ stand on his head.

5. _____ Catherine sleep at your house tonight?

## THE VERBS *LET* AND *LEAVE*

Fill in each blank with the correct form of **let** or **leave**.

1. _____ them stay up a little longer.

2. Don't _____ the plates there.

3. I will not _____ him do that.

4. We _____ the dog alone yesterday.

5. Don _____ the children do that.

GO ON TO THE NEXT PAGE

## THE WORDS *YOUR* AND *YOU'RE*, *ITS* AND *IT'S*, *THEIR* AND *THEY'RE*, AND *WHOSE* AND *WHO'S*

Fill in each blank with the correct word.

1. _____ done this terrible thing? (**Whose** or **Who's**)

2. _____ parents will hear about this? (**Whose** or **Who's**)

3. _____ not welcome here. (**Your** or **You're**)

4. _____ not very nice. (**Its** or **It's**)

5. _____ parents should do something about them. (**Their** or **They're**)

## THE COMMA

Each of the following sentences has two adjectives. Add commas between adjectives when they are needed. If a sentence needs no comma, write **NC** in the blank following the sentence.

1. My beautiful precious child hurt herself before.  _____

2. Katie bought a large black bicycle.  _____

3. The long slimy worm crawled across the floor.  _____

4. Her thick black hair is very pretty.  _____

5. This loud noisy party is getting on my nerves.  _____

## VERB FORMS AS ADJECTIVES

In the blank in each phrase, write the adjective form of the verb.

1. the _____ child (**cry**)

2. the _____ doll (**talk**)

3. the _____ water (**run**)

4. the _____ mother (**work**)

5. the _____ insect (**fly**)

## NOUNS AS ADJECTIVES

Underline the nouns that act as adjectives.

1. ugly white storm door

2. long, sharp kitchen knife

3. thick, creamy chicken soup

GO ON TO THE NEXT PAGE

**4.** nice black steel gate

**5.** the exciting football game

## MISPLACED DESCRIPTIVE PHRASES

The descriptive phrases are misplaced in the following sentences. Write the sentences over with the descriptive phrases in the right places.

**1.** Diane drove her car eating a pear.

_____

**2.** The carpenter fixed the window chewing gum.

_____

**3.** George sat in the chair scratching his head.

_____

**4.** Patrick went into the store wearing shorts.

_____

**5.** Dave left the train carrying a newspaper.

_____

## UNNECESSARY WORDS

Each of the following sentences contains the word **of** unnecessarily. Write each sentence over correctly.

**1.** Please take those shoes off of the bed.

_____

**2.** The men went out of the door just a moment ago.

_____

**3.** We need to buy a half of a pound of cheese.

_____

**4.** Fred lives near me off of Broad Street.

_____

**5.** I will not wait longer than half of an hour for you.

_____

GO ON TO THE NEXT PAGE

# DOUBLE NEGATIVES

The following sentences have double negatives. Write each sentence over so that it has only one negative word. Replace one of the negative words with a positive word.

1. I don't understand nothing.

_____

2. Pablo didn't do nothing.

_____

3. Nobody knows nothing here.

_____

4. The police don't say nothing.

_____

5. This butter isn't no good anymore.

_____

# CONTRACTIONS

Write the contractions for the following.

1. who is  _____

2. we are  _____

3. there is  _____

4. what is  _____

5. it will  _____

6. we will  _____

7. let us  _____

8. they have  _____

9. she has  _____

10. you are  _____

# THE WORDS *A* AND *AN*

Put **a** or **an** before each of the following.

1. _____ heavy load

2. _____ honorable man

3. _____ iron-clad alibi

4. _____ aspirin

5. _____ bank

6. _____ argument

7. _____ eager person

8. _____ earthquake

9. _____ unclaimed ticket

10. _____ cracker

GO ON TO THE NEXT PAGE

## WRITING PARAGRAPHS

Read the following paragraph. Underline the words that help link the sentences.

The sex-education course at my children's junior high school delivers a well-balanced survey of important issues. On one hand, the course gives careful attention to the pleasures and benefits of an intimate sexual relationship. On the other, it cautions about the dangers of irresponsible sex, especially in this day and age. I am glad my children enjoy the course, and I hope it helps them develop attitudes toward sex that makes it a positive part of their lives.

## ORGANIZING SENTENCES INTO A PARAGRAPH

Write the following sentences over in a paragraph that makes sense. First, write the introductory sentence. Then add the other sentences in a logical order.

However, his failing was that he didn't keep his supervisor informed about important events. Mario did all but one of the tasks of his job well. She made the mistake only because Mario had not told her about the change in a certain customer's order. One day his supervisor made a decision that turned out to be very embarrassing. As a result, Mario was put on warning and advised to be careful to relay critical information to his supervisor. He handled the switchboard with ease, entered data into the computer accurately, and dealt well with customers.

_____

_____

_____

_____

_____

_____

_____

_____

_____

GO ON TO THE NEXT PAGE

## SENTENCE VARIETY

Rewrite the following paragraph to make it more pleasing to read.

    I will never forget how I met my wife. I was working in a food store. I was working as a cash register clerk. One day she came into the store. She was with her mother. They came to buy things. I saw her. I fell in love with her right away. Her mother came to my check-out lane. I was delighted. I tried to act very cool. I smiled at both of them. They left the store. I was upset. I felt I would never see the girl of my dreams again. Two days later, a friend invited me to a party. You can imagine my surprise. At the party was the girl of my dreams. I went up to her and said, "Hi." I reminded her that I had seen her before in the food store. The rest is history.

_____

_____

_____

_____

_____

_____

## PROOFREADING

Proofread the following paragraph. Write the whole paragraph over with the mistakes corrected.

    whenevr my freind his brothr and i wold walk down the stret we alway tried to avoid steping on the crack of the sidewak. No one evr said that we should'nt but we just did'nt. once my little sister, who always like to follw us, ran in fron of us. Then she purposely stepped on evry crak in the sidwalk. Somhow my freind his brother and i felt that our luk changd aftr that. i no it sound silly buat nothin went right for us for a long tim.

_____

_____

_____

_____

_____

_____

GO ON TO THE NEXT PAGE

## WRITING AN INVITATION

Write a letter to invite someone to a friendly get-together.

_____

_____

_____

_____

_____

_____

_____

_____

_____

_____

_____

_____

_____

GO ON TO THE NEXT PAGE

**110**

# WRITING A BUSINESS LETTER

Write a letter because you did not receive your sick-pay benefits check. Write to the following address: **New Jersey Department of Labor, 234 East State Street, Trenton, New Jersey 08618.**

GO ON TO THE NEXT PAGE

## SPELLING

Write the correct spelling of each of the following words.

1. reson _____
2. mater _____
3. exersize _____
4. lenth _____
5. lonly _____
6. positon _____
7. acident _____
8. arguement _____
9. beleive _____
10. necesary _____

11. sucseed _____
12. bilding _____
13. espensive _____
14. hieght _____
15. reconize _____
16. opinon _____
17. compony _____
18. calender _____
19. cornor _____
20. skedule _____

## ALPHABETIZING (USING THE DICTIONARY)

Use the guide words **money** and **movie** to answer the questions. Write **Yes** or **No** in each blank.

1. Is the word **motive** on this page? _____
2. Is the word **mountain** on this page? _____
3. Is the word **monster** on this page? _____
4. Is the word **monument** on this page? _____
5. Is the word **movable** on this page? _____

CHECK ANSWERS BEGINNING ON PAGE 131.

Count how many items you answered correctly in each **Section** of the Review. Write your score per section in the **My Scores** column. If all your section scores are as high as the **Good Scores**, you have successfully completed the *Power English* program. If any of your section scores are lower than the **Good Scores**, study the lessons on the assigned **Review Pages** in *Power English 8*.

| Section | Good Scores | My Scores | Review Pages |
|---|---|---|---|
| Capitalizing | 4 or 5 | | 2, 28, 50, 72, 96–97 |
| Singular and Plural Subjects | 4 or 5 | | 3 |
| Recognizing Sentences | 4 or 5 | | 4 |
| Word Order in Sentences | 4 or 5 | | 5, 56, 98 |
| Combining Sentences | 4 or 5 | | 6, 29–30 |
| Shortening Sentences | 4 or 5 | | 8 |
| Sentence Parts (Dependent and Independent Word Groups) | 4 or 5 | | 7, 31 |
| Combining Independent and Dependent Word Groups | 4 or 5 | | 32, 51–52, 73, 74 |
| Direct Quotations | 4 or 5 | | 53 |
| Direct and Indirect Quotations | 4 or 5 | | 54–55 |
| End Marks (Punctuation Marks) | 4 or 5 | | 9 |
| Pronouns and What They Refer To | 4 or 5 | | 33 |
| Pronouns (Showing Ownership or Belonging To) | 4 or 5 | | 10–11 |
| The Words **Each, Either . . . Or,** and **Neither . . . Nor** | 4 or 5 | | 75–76, 99 |
| Adjectives and Adverbs | 4 or 5 | | 34 |
| Regular and Irregular Verbs | 4 or 5 | | 12 |
| Using the Words **Has** and **Have** with Verbs | 4 or 5 | | 13 |

| Section | Good Scores | My Scores | Review Pages |
|---|---|---|---|
| The Verbs **Cut**, **Cuts**, **Will Cut**, **Has Cut**, **Have Cut**, and **Had Cut** | 4 or 5 | | 35 |
| The Verbs **Set** and **Sit** | 4 or 5 | | 58 |
| The Words **Can** and **May** | 4 or 5 | | 77 |
| The Verbs **Let** and **Leave** | 4 or 5 | | 100 |
| The Words **Your** and **You're**, **Its** and **It's**, **Their** and **They're**, and **Whose** and **Who's** | 4 or 5 | | 57 |
| The Comma | 4 or 5 | | 101 |
| Verb Forms as Adjectives | 4 or 5 | | 59 |
| Nouns as Adjectives | 4 or 5 | | 82 |
| Misplaced Descriptive Phrases | 4 or 5 | | 60, 78–79, 102–103 |
| Unnecessary Words | 4 or 5 | | 80–81 |
| Double Negatives | 4 or 5 | | 104–105 |
| Contractions | 8, 9, or 10 | | 36 |
| The Words **A** and **An** | 8, 9, or 10 | | 106 |
| Writing Paragraphs | 2 | | 37 |
| Organizing Sentences into a Paragraph | 6 | | 38–39, 61, 83, 107, 108 |
| Sentence Variety | A correct paragraph | | 84, 109 |
| Proofreading | 33–41 | | 40, 62, 110 |
| Writing an Invitation | A correct letter | | 14–15 |
| Writing a Business Letter | A correct letter | | 85 |
| Spelling | 16–20 | | 16, 41, 63, 86, 111 |
| Alphabetizing (Using the Dictionary) | 4 or 5 | | 17, 42, 64, 87, 112 |

# ANSWERS

# *POWER ENGLISH 1* REVIEW

## Capital Letters (p. 1)

1. Mr. and Mrs. Michael A. Pardini are going on a trip in March.
2. On Thursday Maria and I are visiting our friend Mrs. Mathews.
3. I like the months April, May, and June the best.
4. Herbert K. King and I are leaving in August.
5. Miss Sally A. Daniels and I start work on Monday.

## Telling and Asking Sentences (p. 1)

1. What did he say?
2. No one is here.
3. I refused to go there yesterday.
4. Did you see that?
5. The poor man is hurt.

## Word Order in Sentences (p. 2)

1. My friends are going to a party.
2. How far is it to your house?
3. Do you like your work?
4. Is the poor child lost?
   **or:** Is the lost child poor?
5. The handsome man asked Meg for a dance.
   **or:** Meg asked the handsome man for a dance.

## Naming Words (Nouns) (p. 2)

1. husband
2. work
3. job
4. months
5. house
6. money
7. children
8. clothes
9. school
10. state

## Recognizing Naming Words (Nouns) (p. 3)

You should have a line under the following:

1. child; robber; store
2. brother; food
3. father; brother
4. aunt; person
5. people

## More than One (Plural) (p. 3)

1. three peaches
2. a cookie
3. four camps
4. C
5. two Joneses
6. two branches
7. five crashes
8. C
9. ten roses
10. two Charleses

## Recognizing Action Words (Verbs) (p. 3)

You should have a line under the following verbs.

1. hit
2. called
3. threw
4. yelled
5. kicked

## Action Words (Verbs) (pp. 3–4)

You should have circled the following verbs.

1. dry
2. drives
3. need
4. lives
5. runs

## Action Words (Verbs): Now and Before Now (p. 4)

You should have circled the following verbs.

1. work
2. played
3. barked
4. loves
5. needed

## The Words *Am*, *Are*, and *Is* (p. 4)

1. are
2. am
3. Is
4. are
5. are

## Action Words and Helping Words (Verbs) (p. 4)

1. are
2. am
3. Is
4. are
5. is

## The Words *He*, *She*, *It*, *I*, and *They* (p. 5)

1. He
2. They
3. She; I
4. They
5. It

## Recognizing Describing Words (Adjectives) (p. 5)

You should have a line under the following:

1. beautiful blue
2. large gray; cold
3. charming
4. frightened
5. pretty red; black

## The Words *A* and *An* (p. 5)

1. an old house
2. a sharp knife
3. a hard worker
4. a yellow sweater
5. an easy problem
6. a young child
7. an oak tree
8. an action
9. a cute baby
10. an even score

## Writing a Friendly Letter (p. 6)

Sample letter:

```
                            June 5, 1990
Dear Tara,
   Thank you for inviting me to your
home for dinner. I enjoyed myself very
much. You are an incredible cook.
Everything was delicious.
   I look forward to seeing you again
soon.

                   Your friend,
                   Donna
```

### The Alphabet (p. 6)

| | | |
|---|---|---|
| 1. all | 10. jam | 19. seven |
| 2. book | 11. kit | 20. tree |
| 3. carrot | 12. love | 21. use |
| 4. dark | 13. milk | 22. very |
| 5. enter | 14. no | 23. was |
| 6. fry | 15. out | 24. x-ray |
| 7. girl | 16. park | 25. year |
| 8. help | 17. quiet | 26. zoo |
| 9. ice | 18. ran | |

# POWER ENGLISH 2 REVIEW

### Capitalizing (p. 9)

1. In January Tomiko and I are going to Chicago, Illinois.
2. I love to read stories like "Killer in the Night."
3. Power English helps people gain writing skill.
4. In May Sara is moving to Hardy Drive in Baltimore, Maryland.
5. I just finished reading A Trip to the Moon.

### Telling and Asking Sentences (p. 9)

1. Mr. and Mrs. Torres enjoy reading.
2. Who said that to you?
3. That is an incredible thing to say!
4. What do they want?
5. Don't go.
   **or:** Don't go!

### Asking Sentences (Questions) (p. 10)

Sample answers:
1. When do you read?
   **or:** What do you do at night?
2. Where does Ben live?
3. How do you get to work?
   **or:** What do you ride to work?
4. When did Bernice move to New York City?
   **or:** Where did Bernice move in July?
5. What does Leon love to play?

### End Marks (p. 10)

1. She is a very special person.
2. I can't believe you did that!
3. Who saw them go?
4. This is incredible!
5. Help them.
   **or:** Help them!

### Recognizing Sentences (p. 10)

You should have a check by the following.
3. Do that now.          4. Run faster.

### Sentence Parts (p. 11)

1. **e** A house had fallen.
2. **d** A poor child was trapped.
3. **a** People were working hard to free her.
4. **c** Bricks and wood were on top of the child.
5. **b** It was terrible to watch.

### Word Order in Sentences (p. 11)

1. Everyone needs to be loved.
2. Christine is all alone in the world.
3. No one ever invites her to dinner.
4. She goes to work in the morning.
   **or:** In the morning she goes to work.
5. She comes home to an empty apartment every night.
   **or:** Every night she comes home to an empty apartment.

### The Complete Subject of a Sentence (p. 11)

You should have a line under the following.
1. Ellen and Laura          4. Tara and I
2. The trees                5. They
3. My sisters and brothers

### More Than One (Plural) (p. 12)

| | |
|---|---|
| 1. two boxes | 6. five boys |
| 2. three babies | 7. six axes |
| 3. ten washes | 8. two dummies |
| 4. four hobbies | 9. four doors |
| 5. five ways | 10. two passes |

### The Pronouns I, You, He, She, It, We, and They (p. 12)

1. He      2. It      3. I      4. We      5. They

### Recognizing Describing Words (Adjectives) (p. 12)

You should have a line under the following.
1. old broken             4. silly, unused
2. worn, rusty; large     5. biggest
3. nice; useless

### Describing Words (Adjectives) (p. 13)

1. largest      3. merrier      5. laziest
2. sloppiest    4. deeper

## Action Words (Verbs) (p. 13)

1. argue  3. yell  5. make
2. speaks  4. raises

## Action Words (Verbs): Present, Past, and Future Time (p. 13)

1. hurry  3. needs  5. tried
2. rushed  4. will land

## The Words *Am, Are, Is, Was,* and *Were* (Verbs) (p. 14)

1. am  2. Were  3. are  4. Was  5. is

## The Words *There Is* and *There Are* (p. 14)

1. There is  3. There is  5. There is
2. There are  4. There are

## The Words *Has, Had,* and *Have* (Verbs) (p. 14)

1. have  3. have  5. had
2. has  4. have

## The Words *Do, Does,* and *Did* (Verbs) (p. 14)

1. did  3. Do  5. does
2. do  4. did

## Shortening Words (Contractions) (p. 15)

1. won't  5. hadn't  8. haven't
2. shouldn't  6. hasn't  9. weren't
3. wasn't  7. don't  10. aren't
4. isn't

## The Words *A* and *An* (p. 15)

1. a happy person  6. an iron
2. an orange  7. an hour
3. an honest man  8. an x-ray
4. an honor  9. an ocean
5. a pie  10. a young woman

## Writing a Friendly Letter (p. 15)

Sample letter:

```
                    September 2, 1990
Dear Rita,
    Thank you so much for all your
help. I could never have moved into my
apartment without your help.
    I am glad you are my friend.

                    Your pal,
                    Christine
```

## Addressing an Envelope (p. 16)

Sample envelope:

```
Mary Jane Gates
439 Fifth Avenue
Chicago, Illinois 60601

        Milly Moore
        925 Bates Avenue
        Chicago, Illinois 60620
```

## Spelling (pp. 16–17)

1. I am going to the store at two o'clock, too.
2. Is it right to write her a letter?
3. I don't know why you have no money.
4. I ate an apple at eight o'clock.
5. She can sew dresses so well!
6. I did hear that they were here.
7. Dan read a book about a red house.
8. Will our friend be here in an hour?
9. I can meet you after I buy the meat.
10. He will weigh that on the way home.

## Alphabetizing (p. 17)

1. base, bet, bite, blame, board, broom, busy
2. bank, blame, cream, cute, frame, save, slap
3. farm, feel, fine, flower, fool, frame, full
4. able, act, all, am, are, ask, at
5. tell, the, time, too, track, tune, two

# *POWER ENGLISH 3* REVIEW

## Capitalizing (p. 21)

1. Mr. and Mrs. A. I. Adams live on Spruce Street in Reno, Nevada.
2. Miss Jasper and Ms. Veldez are going to England in the summer.
3. "I am on a Free Ride to Nowhere" is an interesting story.
4. Maria likes funny love poems like "My Heart Is a Marshmallow."
5. Mr. and Mrs. J. L. Zavarelli have lived in Texas, Virginia, Utah, Oregon, and Maine.

## Compound Subjects and Verbs in Sentences (p. 21)

You should have one line under the following.
1. Marcos, Tony  4. man, wife
2. men, dog  5. people
3. they
You should have two lines under the following.
1. quit, traveled  4. offered
2. headed  5. sang, joked
3. gambled, lost

## Sentence Parts (p. 22)

1. e  Travel makes me ill.
2. d  I am not a good traveler.
3. a  My job requires me to travel.
4. b  Many people love to travel.
5. c  They should have my job.

## Recognizing Sentences (p. 22)

You should have a check by the following.
1. Help is on the way.     2. Go immediately.

## Combining Sentences (pp. 22–23)

1. Robert needs, wants, and has help now.
2. Sara types, writes, and speaks well.
3. The lake looks, feels, and smells good.
4. Clara cleans the house, goes to work, and takes care of the children.
5. The movie bothered, frightened, and drained us.

## Shortening Sentences with Commas (p. 23)

1. Richard, Florence, and Julio work hard every day.
2. José, Maria, and Francis usually eat too much at Thanksgiving.
3. Karen, Stanley, and I entered the new store.
4. The small child, dog, and kitten are here now.
5. The new salesperson, boss, and secretary started work on Monday.

## Word Order in Sentences and Commas (p. 24)

1. Stephanie, Dennis, and I work here.
2. Butter, red meat, and cream are high in fat.
3. I love swimming, bowling, and walking.
4. We ate sandwiches, salads, and fruit at the party.
   **or:** At the party we ate sandwiches, salads, and fruit.
5. The police are looking for an escaped prisoner, his wife, and his friend.

## Command Sentences (p. 24)

1. Don't go there.
   **or:** Don't go there!
2. Wait.
   **or:** Wait!
3. Who said that?
4. Walter is very mean.
5. Hurry up.
   **or:** Hurry up!

## Recognizing Naming Words (Nouns) (p. 24)

You should have lines under the following.
   I finally met a person I could fall in love with. However, my luck, he is already married. I will not go out with a married man. He likes me. However, he has a wife. I would not like a woman to do the same thing to me if I were married. He has asked me for dates. It's hard, but I keep saying "No." Why are all the good men married? It is hard being a single woman today.

## More Than One (Plural) (p. 25)

1. children     5. babies     8. mice
2. men          6. feet       9. books
3. teeth        7. women      10. glasses
4. geese

## The Pronouns *I, You, He, She, It, We,* and *They* (p. 25)

1. It     2. They     3. We     4. He     5. I

## The Pronouns *Him* and *Her* (p. 25)

1. him     3. him     5. him
2. She     4. her

## The Pronoun *Them* (p. 26)

1. them     3. them     5. them
2. They     4. They

## Describing Words and Linking Words (p. 26)

You should have a line under the following.
1. nice young; favorite     4. big; tired
2. older; happy; content    5. scary; long
3. charming, handsome; lucky

## Describing Words (Adjectives) (p. 26)

1. taller      3. stupidest     5. loveliest
2. smartest    4. nicer

## Action Words (Verbs) (pp. 26–27)

1. climbed; will climb     4. worked; will work
2. baked; will bake        5. washed; will wash
3. cooked; will cook

## The Verbs *Go, Goes, Went,* and *Will Go* (p. 27)

1. will go     3. goes     5. goes
2. went        4. went

## The Verbs *Has, Have, Had,* and *Will Have* (p. 27)

1. Have
2. will have
3. had
4. has
5. will have

## The Verbs *Do, Does, Did,* and *Will Do* (p. 27)

1. did
2. do
3. will do
4. did
5. do

## The Verbs *See, Sees, Saw,* and *Will See* (p. 28)

1. will see
2. saw
3. see
4. saw
5. sees

## Recognizing Describing Words (Adverbs) (p. 28)

You should have a line under the following.
1. fast
2. yesterday
3. brightly
4. terribly
5. immediately

## Describing Words (Adverbs) (p. 28)

1. terribly
2. nicely
3. quickly
4. carefully
5. cruelly
6. horribly
7. cheerfully
8. slowly
9. happily
10. sadly

## Writing the Time of Day (p. 28)

1. 2:10 A.M.
2. 9:05 P.M.
3. 3:20 P.M.
4. 11:15 A.M.
5. 8:30 P.M.

## Writing Dates (p. 29)

1. August 10, 1929
2. June 3, 1988
3. February 11, 1954
4. October 10, 1955
5. May 4, 1952

## Writing Addresses (p. 29)

1. 912 Carter Road
   Chicago, Illinois
   60610

2. 213 Main Street
   Syracuse, New York
   13220

## Shortening Words (Contractions) (p. 29)

1. can't
2. I'll
3. they're
4. I'm
5. we've
6. haven't
7. she's
8. couldn't
9. he's
10. won't

## The Words *A* and *An* (p. 29)

1. an honest person
2. an hour
3. an unusual sight
4. an early date
5. a union
6. an empire
7. a house
8. a usual thing
9. a happy child
10. an ugly picture

## Using *Yes* and *No* in a Sentence (p. 30)

1. Yes, I will help you.
2. No, he is not here now.
3. Yes, they were here earlier.
4. Yes, I know them well.
5. No, I do not like them.

## Writing an Invitation (p. 30)

Sample invitation:

```
                        September 4, 1990
Dear Pedro,
   I am having a get-together of a few
people on Friday, September 17, at 8:00
P.M. at my home. It's informal, so
dress comfortably. I'll supply the food
and drink. Come prepared to have fun.
   Please phone me at 555-8645 by
September 12.

                   Your friend,
                   Keung
```

## Addressing an Envelope (p. 31)

Sample envelope:

```
Keung Ling
674 Winter Drive
Dallas, Texas 75220

          Pedro Veldez
          21 George Street
          Dallas, Texas 75202
```

## Spelling (p. 31)

1. hoping; hoped
2. canning; canned
3. trapping; trapped
4. jumping; jumped
5. dropping; dropped
6. hopping; hopped
7. pinning; pinned
8. looking; looked
9. chopping; chopped
10. dining; dined

## Spelling (p. 32)

1. The fair man said he did not have any bus fare.
2. I do not know if that is the right way to the fair.

## Alphabetizing (p. 32)

Allan Brandeis, Joseph Bryant, Alice Cracker, Francis Cruel, George Doll, Dorothy Dome, Edward Donne, Frank Dorm, Sylvia Dram, Sara Dreber, Tara Driem, Julio Droom, Kathy Drum, Sally Dryer, Davis Foyer

**121**

**Alphabetizing (Using the Dictionary) (p. 32)**

1. Yes   2. Yes   3. Yes   4. Yes   5. No

## *POWER ENGLISH 4* REVIEW

**Capitalizing (Common Nouns and Proper Nouns) (p. 35)**

1. grapes
2. Atlantic Ocean
3. Mr. Marrero
4. winter
5. Dave C. Ridgley
6. Memorial Day
7. fruit
8. Halloween
9. Independence Day
10. Labor Day
11. Ohio
12. city
13. teacher
14. C
15. autumn
16. Christmas
17. bedroom
18. day
19. number
20. labor

**Singular and Plural Subjects (p. 35)**

1. P   3. S   5. S   7. P   9. S
2. P   4. P   6. P   8. P   10. P

**Sentence Parts (p. 36)**

1. **c**   There are eight people in my family.
2. **a**   I have four brothers and one sister.
3. **b**   My sister, Patricia, sleeps in the living room.
4. **e**   We all still live at home.
5. **d**   My parents work very hard.

**Recognizing Sentences (p. 36)**

You should have a check by the following.
1. Stop talking.          5. Do not go there now.

**Word Order in Sentences (p. 36)**

1. My sister, brother, and I work in the same place.
2. My favorite flowers are tulips, roses, and pansies.
   **or:** Tulips, roses, and pansies are my favorite
   flowers.

**End Marks (p. 36)**

1. Hurry up.
   **or:** Hurry up!
2. Stand still.
3. Is that the truth?
4. Ken tries hard.
5. Yes, I will go tomorrow.

**Writing Sentences with Compound Subjects (p. 37)**

Sample sentences:
1. The train and car hit one another.
2. The men, women, and children ran to get out of the rain.

**Combining Sentences (p. 37)**

1. George won a great battle and found a reason to live.
2. He had been very ill and had almost given up.
3. His family supported him and stayed by him.
4. They gave him courage and refused to let him die.
5. George beat all the odds and is now a famous ballplayer.

**Combining Sentences (p. 38)**

1. Life is precious, must be lived to its fullest, and should not be wasted.
2. Every person needs love, understanding, and belonging.
3. Happiness, love, and belonging cannot be bought.
4. The small child had fallen in a well, broken her leg, and twisted her neck.
5. The firemen, police, and rescue squad tried to get the child out of the well.

**Shortening Sentences with Commas (p. 39)**

1. All the letters, packages, and stamps were stolen from the mail carrier.
2. Jeff, Marcella, Hideo, and I are best friends.
3. Peter worked as a delivery boy, clerk, and salesperson.
4. The brave man rushed into the burning building, ran up the stairs, and rescued the infant.
5. The men, women, and children screamed with joy.

**Adjectives (Describing Words) (p. 39)**

1. longest        3. healthier      5. cleanest
2. lazier         4. dirtiest

**Adjectives (Describing Words) and Linking Words (p. 40)**

1. prettier **or** smarter      4. cleverest
2. smarter **or** prettier      5. good
3. happy

**The Pronouns *I, You, He, She, It, We,* and *They* (p. 40)**

1. It     2. We     3. I     4. He     5. It

**The Pronouns *Me, Him, Her, Us,* and *Them* (p. 40)**

1. him     2. I     3. me     4. us     5. They

## More Than One (Noun Plurals) (p. 41)

1. shelves
2. wives
3. tables
4. teeth
5. knives
6. safes
7. mice
8. cherries
9. feet
10. loaves

## Agreement of Subject and Verb (p. 41)

You should have a line under the following.

1. falls
2. looks
3. love
4. like
5. go

## Verbs (Action Words): Present Time (p. 41)

1. arrives
2. play
3. eat
4. do
5. go

## The Verbs *Run, Runs, Ran,* and *Will Run* (p. 41)

1. will run
2. runs
3. ran
4. ran
5. run

## The Verbs *Eat, Eats, Ate,* and *Will Eat* (p. 42)

1. ate
2. eat
3. Eat
4. will eat
5. will eat

## The Verbs *Take, Takes, Took,* and *Will Take* (p. 42)

1. take
2. took
3. will take
4. will take
5. took

## The Verbs *Grow, Grows, Grew,* and *Will Grow* (p. 42)

1. grew
2. will grow
3. grew
4. grows
5. grow

## Adverbs (Describing Words) (p. 42)

1. soon **or** tomorrow
2. here
3. down
4. tomorrow **or** soon
5. today

## Adverbs (Describing Words) (p. 43)

Sample answers:

1. very
2. quite
3. very
4. too
5. very

## The Words *Good* and *Well* (p. 43)

1. good
2. well
3. well
4. good
5. well

## Showing Ownership or Belonging To (Possession) (p. 43)

1. wives, wives'
2. feet, feet's
3. safes, safes'
4. passes, passes'
5. matches, matches'
6. shelves, shelves'
7. babies, babies'
8. children, children's
9. churches, churches'
10. cars, cars'

## Contractions (Shortening Words) (p. 44)

1. won't
2. she's
3. they're
4. we'll
5. I'll
6. I've
7. can't
8. doesn't
9. they'll
10. she's

## Commas in Dates and Addresses (p. 44)

1. May 21, 1991
2. Theodore Marcus
   325 Ford Avenue
   New York, New York 10022
3. August 3, 1965
4. September 10, 1947
5. Linda Roth
   42 Jefferson Drive
   Philadelphia, Pennsylvania 19150

## Writing the Time of Day (p. 44)

1. 10:30 P.M.
2. 11:15 P.M.
3. 1:10 A.M.
4. 6:25 P.M.
5. 10:20 A.M.

## The Words *A* and *An* (p. 45)

1. a used van
2. a huge tool
3. a hole
4. a water bottle
5. an answer
6. a uniform
7. a house
8. a year
9. a tray
10. an elephant

## Writing an Invitation (p. 45)

Sample letter:

```
                              October 4, 1990
Dear Nora,

   I am inviting a few people to my home
on Saturday, October 15, at 8:30 P.M. I
would love for you to come. It's just a
little get-together.
   Please phone by October 11 to let me
know if you can make it.

                        Your friend,
                        Nina
```

## Addressing an Envelope (p. 45)

Sample envelope:

```
Nina Bielski
411 Ferris Road
Houston, Texas 77070

            Nora Alba
            56 Rodeo Drive
            Houston, Texas 77079
```

## Spelling (p. 46)

1. business
2. always
3. forty
4. pretty
5. Saturday
6. February
7. country
8. yesterday
9. guess
10. answer
11. a lot
12. already
13. friend
14. Wednesday
15. write
16. woman
17. some
18. doctor
19. Tuesday
20. dear

## Alphabetizing (Using the Dictionary) (p. 46)

1. No   2. Yes   3. Yes   4. Yes   5. Yes

# POWER ENGLISH 5 REVIEW

## Capitalizing (p. 49)

1. My Aunt Barbara and Uncle Derrick live in the West and are moving east.
2. My cousin lives in West Berlin and is coming to visit us in the United States of America.
3. My Uncle Charles fought in both World War II and the Korean War.
4. Her Aunt Monica is from Italy and speaks Italian, Spanish, and French.
5. Our Chinese friend can speak English, Russian, and Chinese well.

## Singular and Plural Subjects (p. 49)

1. P    3. P    5. P    7. P    9. P
2. S    4. P    6. P    8. P    10. S

## Sentence Parts (p. 50)

1. d  Stan Flemming was used to hard times.
2. a  His parents were both alcoholics.
3. b  Christmas was just another day.
4. e  Often they didn't even have a tree.
5. c  His brothers and he have been on their own for years.

## End Marks (p. 50)

1. Please show that to me.
2. Is that all you want?
3. How can you do these things?
4. That is wonderful!
5. Move.
   or: Move!

## Agreement of Subject and Verb (p. 50)

You should have a line under the following.

1. want      3. see      5. is
2. works     4. need

## Combining Sentences (pp. 50–51)

1. My wife started work today and likes her job.
2. Our children go to a friend's house and stay there all day.
3. My daughter, son, and friend's son play outside in our friend's yard.
4. Our friend's yard has swings, a sand box, and a jungle gym.
5. My daughter, son, and friend's son like it at our friend's house.

## Shortening Sentences (p. 51)

1. C
2. Jamie, Al, and Donald worry all the time.
3. Jamie needs more money, time, and work.
4. C
5. Al, his wife, and his son complain a lot.

## Pronouns (pp. 51–52)

1. me    3. him    5. them    7. her    9. us
2. I     4. her    6. us      8. me     10. him

## Pronouns (Showing Ownership or Belonging To) (p. 52)

1. mine   2. his   3. Its   4. hers   5. theirs

## Pronouns and What They Refer To (pp. 52–53)

1. It        5. She          8. her
2. They      6. his or her   9. its
3. We        7. their        10. his
4. He

## Adjectives (p. 53)

1. most stubborn
2. friendlier
3. older
4. most charming
5. quieter

## Adjectives and Linking Words (p. 53)

| 1. pretty | 3. nice | 5. fresher |
|---|---|---|
| 2. unluckiest | 4. tired | |

## The Verbs *Bite*, *Bites*, *Bit*, and *Will Bite* (p. 54)

| 1. bit | 3. bit | 5. bit |
|---|---|---|
| 2. bites | 4. will bite | |

## The Verbs *Get*, *Gets*, *Got*, and *Will Get* (p. 54)

| 1. gets | 3. gets | 5. got |
|---|---|---|
| 2. Get | 4. will get | |

## The Verbs *Begin*, *Begins*, *Began*, and *Will Begin* (p. 54)

| 1. will begin | 3. begins | 5. began |
|---|---|---|
| 2. began | 4. Begin | |

## The Verbs *Know*, *Knows*, *Knew*, and *Will Know* (p. 54)

| 1. knows | 3. will know | 5. knew |
|---|---|---|
| 2. knew | 4. will know | |

## The Verbs *Drink*, *Drinks*, *Drank*, and *Will Drink* (p. 55)

| 1. Drink | 3. will drink | 5. drank |
|---|---|---|
| 2. drinks | 4. will drink | |

## Adverbs (p. 55)

| 1. faster | 3. later | 5. slowest |
|---|---|---|
| 2. wilder | 4. earliest | |

## Showing Ownership or Belonging To (Possession) (p. 55)

| 1. Jameses, Jameses' | 6. wives, wives' |
|---|---|
| 2. dresses, dresses' | 7. watches, watches' |
| 3. children, children's | 8. men, men's |
| 4. boxes, boxes' | 9. ladies, ladies' |
| 5. mice, mice's | 10. houses, houses' |

## The Words *Its* and *It's* (p. 56)

| 1. its | 3. Its | 5. its |
|---|---|---|
| 2. It's | 4. it's | |

## The Words *Their* and *They're* (p. 56)

| 1. Their | 3. they're | 5. Their |
|---|---|---|
| 2. their | 4. They're | |

## The Words *Your* and *You're* (p. 56)

| 1. your | 3. your | 5. you're |
|---|---|---|
| 2. You're | 4. Your | |

## Contractions (p. 56)

| 1. I'm | 5. she'll | 8. it'll |
|---|---|---|
| 2. I'll | 6. they're | 9. they've |
| 3. he's | 7. it's | 10. we've |
| 4. it's | | |

## The Words *A* and *An* (p. 57)

| 1. an honest lady | 6. an early bird |
|---|---|
| 2. an unused jar | 7. an aide |
| 3. an hour | 8. an owner |
| 4. a used car | 9. a hen |
| 5. an aunt | 10. an uncle |

## Writing an Invitation (p. 57)

Sample letter:

December 4, 1990

Dear Peggy,

I am having a Christmas party at my home and would like you to come. The party is on Sunday, December 17, at 2:00 P.M.

Please phone by December 11, to let me know if you will be able to come to my party. I'm looking forward to seeing you.

Your friend,
Janet

## Writing a Business Letter (p. 58)

Sample letter:

532 Grant Avenue
Baltimore, Maryland 21231
May 11, 1990

Michael Rivera, President
ACE Lumber Company
411 Grover Road
Baltimore, Maryland 21229

Dear Mr. Rivera:

I have been charged four times for material I have not received. Your billing department promised it would take care of the problem, but the bills keep coming. Please phone as soon as possible so that we can straighten this out. My phone number is 555-9861.

Thank you for your help.

Sincerely yours,
Anthony Brown

## Addressing an Envelope (p. 59)

```
Anthony Brown
532 Grant Avenue
Baltimore, Maryland 21231

        Mr. Michael Rivera, President
        ACE Lumber Company
        411 Grover Road
        Baltimore, Maryland 21229
```

## Spelling (p. 59)

| | | |
|---|---|---|
| 1. prize | 8. where | 15. sugar |
| 2. tonight | 9. tomorrow | 16. nineteen |
| 3. separate | 10. ninety | 17. truly |
| 4. every | 11. today | 18. teacher |
| 5. believe | 12. January | 19. minute |
| 6. often | 13. choose | 20. trouble |
| 7. clothes | 14. easy | |

## Alphabetizing (Using the Dictionary) (p. 60)

1. Yes  2. No  3. Yes  4. Yes  5. No

## *POWER ENGLISH 6* REVIEW

## Capitalizing (p. 63)

| | |
|---|---|
| 1. C | 6. Mother Theresa |
| 2. C | 7. Aunt Margaret |
| 3. Moore Computers | 8. C |
| 4. Drake Carpenters | 9. C |
| 5. Disneyland | 10. Sears Building |

## Singular and Plural Subjects (p. 63)

You should have a line under the following.

| | |
|---|---|
| 1. apartment (S) | 4. teeth (P) |
| 2. girl, boy (P) | 5. parents (P) |
| 3. buttons (P) | |

## Agreement of Subject and Verb (p. 63)

You should have a line under the following.

| | | |
|---|---|---|
| 1. has | 3. are | 5. are |
| 2. want | 4. needs | |

## Combining Sentences (p. 64)

1. José, Peter, and Janet have their own used cars.
2. Holly, Jeff, and Sally rent their own apartments today.
3. Ruth, Pat, and Kim love their husbands a lot.
4. Lisa, Albert, and Sharon do their jobs very well.
5. My boss, my friend, and I know our drinking limits well.

## Combining Sentences (p. 65)

Sample sentences:
1. We are looking for a new home, but we can't find one we can afford.
2. We have to find one soon, or our furniture will be out in the street.
3. I don't want us to live in a shelter, and our parents have no room for us.
   **or:** I don't want us to live in a shelter, but my parents have no room for us.
4. I look for a place every day, and my wife does all she can.
5. Our children will stay with a friend, but my wife and I will stay at the shelter.
   **or:** Our children will stay with a friend, and my wife and I will stay at the shelter.

## Combining Sentences (p. 65)

1. The shelter is a dangerous place, and people rob you there.
2. C
3. It is depressing to have to be in a shelter, and I hate it there.
4. C
5. Many poor people could once afford to rent, but now they have to live in a shelter.

## Direct Quotations (p. 66)

1. My girlfriend asked, "Are we getting married soon?"
2. Rodrico said, "I need to go back to school."
3. Cheryl asked, "Why are you going to do that?"
4. Diane asked, "Why should I wait for you?"
5. The child said, "That man is running after me."

## Direct and Indirect Quotations (p. 66)

1. She said that she is very happy with her used car.
2. James said that he enjoys his work.
3. The woman said that this man just stole her bag.
4. Brian said that Allison and Joy were arriving soon.
5. Charles said that Mr. Williams is a nice man.

## The Pronouns *Anybody, Anyone, Everybody, Everyone, Nobody, No One, Somebody,* and *Someone* (p. 67)

You should have a line under the following.

| | | |
|---|---|---|
| 1. knows | 3. has | 5. wants |
| 2. is | 4. is | |

## Pronouns (Showing Ownership or Belonging To) (p. 67)

| | | |
|---|---|---|
| 1. mine | 3. His | 5. Its |
| 2. her | 4. their; theirs | |

## Pronouns and What They Refer To (p. 67)

1. its
2. their
3. his
4. her
5. its

## The Pronouns *Who*, *Whom*, and *Whose* (p. 68)

1. whom
2. Whose
3. Who
4. whom
5. Who

## End Marks (Punctuation) (p. 68)

1. He asked whether he could see the ring.
2. Benjamin asked all about you.
3. That is terrible!
4. Why are you doing this?
5. I asked who was going to be at the party.

## Adjectives (p. 68)

1. more
2. many
3. best
4. better
5. most

## Regular and Irregular Verbs (p. 68)

1. helped
2. went
3. knew
4. dried
5. had
6. did
7. bit
8. ran
9. played
10. forgot

## The Verbs *Catch*, *Catches*, *Caught*, and *Will Catch* (p. 69)

1. caught
2. will catch
3. catches
4. Catch
5. catches

## Using the Words *Has* and *Have* with Verbs (p. 69)

1. have gone
2. has helped
3. searched
4. played
5. has worked

## Adding *ing* to Verbs with a Helping Verb (p. 69)

1. am buying
2. is coming
3. are stopping
4. are putting
5. are going

## The Verb *Be* (p. 70)

1. have been
2. were
3. will be
4. are
5. was

## The Verbs *Forget*, *Forgets*, *Forgot*, *Will Forget*, and *Forgotten* (p. 70)

1. forgot
2. have forgotten
3. forgets
4. forgot
5. will forget

## Adverbs (p. 70)

1. more proudly
2. most carelessly
3. most beautifully
4. more quickly
5. more terribly

## The Words *Well*, *Better*, and *Best* (pp. 70–71)

1. well
2. better
3. best
4. better
5. well

## Showing Ownership or Belonging To (Possession) (p. 71)

1. dress's
2. men's
3. boxes'
4. wolves'
5. wife's
6. Charles's
7. children's
8. boys'
9. house's
10. wives'

## The Comma (p. 71)

1. This poor, hardworking woman needs help.
2. NC
3. NC
4. Drink this nice, fresh milk.
5. NC

## Contractions (pp. 71–72)

1. I am; they have
2. will not; she is
3. I have; it is
4. It will; she has
5. They will; we have

## The Words *A* and *An* (p. 72)

1. a healthy person
2. an ear
3. a holy man
4. an x-ray
5. an aisle
6. an ocean
7. an aunt
8. a deer
9. an answer
10. a usual thing

## Writing an Invitation (p. 72)

Sample letter:

> September 4, 1990
>
> Dear Patricio,
>
> We are giving a surprise anniversary party for Miguel and Ines Galvez on Saturday, September 17. The party will be at our house, and we are asking everyone to arrive by 8:00 P.M. The Galvezes will be arriving at 8:20.
>
> Please phone by September 12 so that we can give you more details.
>
> Your friends,
> Victor and Eva

## Writing a Business Letter (p. 73)

Sample letter:

```
                    278 Ewing Street
                    Cambridge, Massachusetts 02142
                    August 1, 1990

Mary Kelly
Windsor School District
368 Brook Drive
Boston, Massachusetts 02115

Dear Ms. Kelly:

   I am answering your ad in the
Courier Post for a bus driver. I am an
experienced driver with an excellent
driving record. In addition, I am
dependable and trustworthy, and I love
children.
   I look forward to hearing from you.
My home phone number is 555-2512.

              Sincerely yours,
              Evelyn Brown
```

## Spelling (p. 74)

1. please
2. loose
3. Thanksgiving
4. holiday
5. beginning
6. sentence
7. niece
8. finally
9. written
10. sincerely
11. quiet
12. until
13. favorite
14. turkey
15. enough
16. excellent
17. science
18. vegetables
19. Thursday
20. marriage

## Alphabetizing (Using the Phone Book) (p. 74)

1. Yes    2. Yes    3. Yes    4. No    5. No

# POWER ENGLISH 7 REVIEW

## Capitalizing (p. 77)

1. C
2. C
3. West Berlin
4. history
5. autumn
6. senator
7. season
8. Uncle Joe
9. company
10. Chinese

## Singular and Plural Subjects (p. 77)

You should have a line under the following.
1. sisters (P)
2. Nobody (S)
3. dog (S)
4. Everybody (S)
5. Someone (S)

## Recognizing Sentences (p. 77)

You should have a check by the following.
3. Stop.              4. My friend is not here.

## Word Order in Sentences (p. 78)

1. José, Karen, Ben, Ann, and I went into business together.
2. We would shop, clean, cook, and babysit for our customers.
3. Everything went well until we began arguing over money.
4. The men felt that they should get paid more than the women.
   or: The women felt that they should get paid more than the men.
5. I said that we should all get equal pay for equal work.

## Combining Sentences (pp. 78–79)

1. Jim's friend is a drug addict, but Jim is not.
2. They have been friends since kindergarten, but Jim cannot put up with his friend's drug problem.
3. Jim's friend must give up drugs, or Jim will no longer be his friend.
4. Jim's friend uses other drug addicts' needles, and they use his needle.
5. Drug addicts think it's a sign of friendship to share needles, but Jim thinks it's a death wish.

## Shortening Sentences (p. 79)

1. My sisters Sharon, Carol, and Jennifer are visiting me tomorrow.
2. My pals Fred, Jay, and Sean are nice.
3. Lynn put on her new coat, gloves, and hat.
4. The train, bus, and van are late today.
5. The man, woman, and child were injured on the bus earlier.

## Sentence Parts (p. 79)

You should have a line under the following.
1. After I buy something good.
4. When they told us the truth.
You should have a check by the following.
2. The men refused to go.
3. Help.
5. Stop that.

128

## Sentence Parts (Dependent and Independent Word Groups) (p. 80)

You should have underlined the following parts of the sentences.

1. She became my best friend <u>after she got out of jail</u>.
2. She made a mistake <u>when she was very young</u>.
3. <u>If people would let her forget</u>, she could begin again.
4. <u>Unless she gets a decent job</u>, she will not make it.
5. She learned many things <u>while she was in prison</u>.

## Direct Quotations (p. 80)

1. Josh asked, "Why won't people help her?"
2. Sandy said, "It's because people do not trust her."
3. Rodrico asked, "What will happen to her?"
4. Ann asked, "Why do people have to be so mean?"
5. Peter said, "Many people have been hurt by being too trusting."

## Direct and Indirect Quotations (pp. 80–81)

1. Florence said, "I am very happy to have such a nice family."
2. Bill said, "I need another good rating from my boss."
3. Betty said, "This is one of the best things I have ever done."
4. Andrew said, "I need all the help I can get."
5. Franco said, "I never worked so hard in all my life."

## End Marks (Punctuation Marks) (p. 81)

1. Barbara asked where they were going.
2. Larry said that he needed another job.
3. What happened to your old job?
4. He said that he and his boss had a fight.
5. Eleni asked how you could get into a fight with your boss.

## Pronouns (p. 81)

1. I, them
2. He, her
3. We, them
4. They, us
5. She, him

## Pronouns and What They Refer To (p. 81)

1. his
2. its
3. their
4. my
5. our

## Pronouns (Showing Ownership or Belonging To) (p. 82)

1. mine
2. theirs
3. its
4. his
5. hers

## The Pronouns *Anybody, Anyone, Everybody, Everyone, Nobody, No One, Somebody,* and *Someone* (p. 82)

You should have a line under the following.

1. wants
2. was
3. is
4. knows
5. has

## The Words *Who, Whom,* and *Whose* (p. 82)

1. Who
2. whom
3. Whose
4. Who
5. whom

## More Than One (Plural) (p. 83)

1. wives
2. children
3. policemen
4. deer
5. feet
6. leaves
7. boxes
8. sheep
9. mice
10. teeth

## Adjectives and Linking Verbs (p. 83)

1. brightest
2. better
3. delicious
4. happier
5. handsome

## Regular and Irregular Verbs (p. 83)

1. changed; has changed
2. called; has called
3. answered; has answered
4. talked; has talked
5. worked; has worked
6. went; has gone
7. stole; has stolen
8. wrote; has written
9. lay; has lain
10. spoke; has spoken

## The Verb *Be* (p. 84)

1. will be
2. was
3. has been
4. was
5. is

## The Verbs *Speak, Speaks, Spoke, Will Speak, Has Spoken, Have Spoken,* and *Had Spoken* (p. 84)

1. will speak
2. spoke
3. spoken
4. spoken
5. speaks

## The Verbs *Steal, Steals, Stole, Will Steal, Has Stolen, Have Stolen,* and *Had Stolen* (p. 84)

1. stolen
2. stolen
3. will steal
4. stole
5. stolen

## The Verbs *Write, Writes, Wrote, Will Write, Has Written, Have Written,* and *Had Written* (p. 84)

1. written
2. wrote
3. will write
4. writes
5. wrote

## The Verbs *Lay, Lays, Laid, Will Lay, Has Laid, Have Laid,* and *Had Laid* (p. 85)

1. laid
2. laid
3. lays
4. will lay
5. Lay

## The Verbs *Lie, Lies, Lay, Will Lie, Has Lain, Have Lain,* and *Had Lain* (p. 85)

1. lain
2. lay
3. lies
4. lain
5. lain

## The Verbs *Teach* and *Learn* (p. 85)

1. taught
2. learned
3. learns
4. will teach
5. learned

## Adverbs (p. 85)

1. worse
2. best
3. hardest
4. sillier **or** more silly
5. higher

## Showing Ownership or Belonging To (Possession) (p. 86)

1. children's
2. deer's
3. Jones's
4. church's
5. wife's

## The Words *Its* and *It's, Their* and *They're,* and *Whose* and *Who's* (p. 86)

1. Whose
2. its
3. it's
4. Who's
5. They're

## The Comma (p. 86)

1. Indeed, that is a cute little black kitten.
2. The big fat cat, however, is angry.
3. For example, the large, mean brown dog growled and jumped at us.
4. NC
5. Of course, we were very grateful.

(Remember, there are no commas before adjectives that refer to size, color, or age.)

## Abbreviations (Shortened Words) (pp. 86–87)

1. Dr.; Ave.
2. Rev.; St.
3. Dr.; Co.; Rd.
4. Rev.; Blvd.; A.M.
5. Dr.; P.M.

## Contractions (p. 87)

1. we've
2. I'm
3. they'll
4. she's
5. can't
6. he's
7. shouldn't
8. I'll
9. won't
10. don't

## Writing the Time of Day (p. 87)

1. 12:35 A.M.
2. 4:45 P.M.
3. 10:25 P.M.
4. 9:10 P.M.
5. 6:30 A.M.
6. 7:05 P.M.
7. 11:05 A.M.
8. 6:25 A.M.
9. 7:30 A.M.
10. 2:30 P.M.

## The Words *A* and *An* (p. 87)

1. an orphan
2. an orange
3. an error
4. a van
5. a pretty girl
6. an honor
7. an apartment
8. a hole
9. an honest mistake
10. a foolish person

## Writing Paragraphs (p. 88)

You should have a line under the following words.

Last year was not the best year of our lives. First, my husband lost his job. Then he became very ill. Eventually, we lost all our money trying to save him, and I had to give up my job to take care of him. Finally, the worst blow of all came when we were put out of our apartment, and we had to go on welfare.

## Organizing Sentences into a Paragraph (p. 88)

Nate and Mia felt miserable on their way to the train station. Thanks to the army, they were going to be separated for the first time in their married lives. At first the army had told Nate that he would never be given a peacetime assignment that would separate him from his wife. Later he was allowed to turn down a certain assignment because it would have meant leaving Mia behind. Finally, however, he got orders to take the assignment he had turned down. As a result, Nate was angry that the army did not keep its promise. Moreover, he was uncomfortable about being separated from his wife for several months.

## Sentence Variety (p. 89)

Sample paragraph:

My father, mother, sister, and I are hard workers. When my sister and I were young, our family was on welfare. Because our parents wanted to get off welfare, they each found and worked on two jobs. They encouraged my sister and me to work and to save money as soon as we were old enough. My sister and I continue to work hard, following our parents' example.

## Proofreading (p. 89)

This is the paragraph as you should have written it. The words and punctuation that were changed are in dark type.

    Stuart is the <u>oldest</u> child in his <u>family</u>. He is hardly out of his <u>teens</u>, but he <u>has</u> been <u>working</u> for a number of <u>years</u> to help out his <u>family</u>. He <u>has</u> had many jobs, <u>and</u> he has never let anyone down. <u>Now</u> he is in college and <u>supporting</u> <u>himself</u>. <u>His</u> <u>family</u> is very proud of <u>him</u>.

## Writing an Invitation (p. 90)

Sample letter:

```
                          May 5, 1990
Dear Marianne,

  My mother and I are giving a bridal
shower for Victoria on Sunday, May 22,
at 3:00 P.M. and would love for you to
attend.
  The party will be at my mother's
house on 32 Harding Lane. Please phone
either my mother at 555-8761 or me at
555-0979 by May 17 to tell us if you
will be joining us.

                    Your friend,
                    Marisol Reyes
```

## Writing a Business Letter (p. 91)

Sample letter:

```
                1034 Tremont Avenue
                Bronx, New York 10450
                December 5, 1990

President
Harper's Department Store
156 Broadway
New York, New York 10003

Dear Sir or Madam:

  I ordered gloves advertised by you in
the Daily News, but I received the
wrong gloves. I sent them back, but I
never received another pair. I now have
neither my money nor my gloves.
  If I do not hear from you soon, I
will give my complaint to the Better
Business Bureau. You can reach me at
the above address. My phone number is
555-8965.

                    Sincerely yours,
                    Bernice Kraft
```

## Spelling (p. 92)

1. only
2. cousin
3. again
4. color
5. because
6. since
7. sometimes
8. health
9. develop
10. instead
11. name
12. picnic
13. good-bye
14. cough
15. receive
16. shoes
17. ache
18. straight
19. judgment
20. just

## Alphabetizing (Using the Phone Book) (p. 92)

1. No
2. No
3. No
4. Yes
5. Yes

# POWER ENGLISH 8 REVIEW

## Capitalizing (p. 97)

1. Bill said, "I am visiting my mother at 6:30 P.M."
2. Marianne asked, "Does she live near us on Sherry Rd.?"
3. Nicole asked whether we were meeting later at the Perry Co.
4. Eric said, "I am going north soon to meet my friends at their house on Dover Ave."
5. Dr. Nettleton and Rev. Henry Nixon are meeting at 9:30 A.M.

## Singular and Plural Subjects (p. 97)

You should have a line under the following.
1. Everybody (S)
2. neighbors (P)
3. car (S)
4. Nobody (S)
5. Tim, I (P)

## Recognizing Sentences (p. 97)

You should have a check by the following.
2. No one can live here.
4. Where did you say you went?

## Word Order in Sentences (p. 98)

1. Sally, Fred, Carmela, and I are starting school again on Monday.
   **or:** On Monday, Sally, Fred, Carmela, and I are starting school again.
2. We are taking courses in English, mathematics, history, and computers.
3. In order to find jobs, we need to gain some skills.
   **or:** We need to gain some skills in order to find jobs.
4. I am going to school because I want to become a secretary.
   **or:** Because I want to become a secretary, I am going to school.
5. A secretary needs to be able to read, speak, and write well.

## Combining Sentences (p. 98)

1. Patience is very important, but sometimes it is hard to be patient.
2. Some people have a lot, but they are never satisfied.
3. Some people have very little, and they have nothing to look forward to.
4. Life can be a great adventure, or it can be a nightmare.
5. Approach life with a positive attitude, or it will wear you down.

## Shortening Sentences (p. 99)

1. Raimundo, Daniella, and Hossein are my good friends.
2. Romain, Yuriko, and Paolo like their coffee hot.
3. I will meet Rosa, King, and Tran later.
4. Gordon, Robin, and Monique are very excited.
5. Donna, Alma, and Akemi have nice apartments.

## Sentence Parts (Dependent and Independent Word Groups) (p. 99)

You should have a line under the following.
1. because they want to get better jobs
2. when he was sixteen years old
3. because he is not happy
4. Until he learns to read, write, and speak better
5. if he really wants to do so

## Combining Independent and Dependent Word Groups (p. 100)

1. When the terrorist boarded the plane, he had a gun.
2. As he walked up and down the aisle, the terrorist pointed the gun at people.
3. The passengers were very frightened because the terrorist looked crazy.
4. Unless the pilot flew him to his homeland, the terrorist would kill the passengers.
5. After the terrorist shot a passenger, the pilot jumped out of his seat and disarmed him.

## Direct Quotations (pp. 100–101)

1. Cleo said, "That is really a very good idea."
2. Howard asked, "Why are you always so late?"
3. Orlando asked, "Is it wise to do this now?"
4. Ellen said, "It seemed fine to me."
5. Fung asked, "Did you finish the job yet?"

## Direct and Indirect Quotations (p. 101)

1. Judy said, "I want to help the poor."
2. Florence said, "My brothers are fine gentlemen."
3. Mrs. Adams said, "My son needs help."
4. Mr. O'Connell said, "I like the people at work."
5. Mrs. Ramirez said, "My husband is doing well."

## End Marks (Punctuation Marks) (p. 101)

1. Robert asked why we are not going tonight.
2. The twins are doing well now.
3. Is that really your house?
4. Why are you being so mean?
5. Elias asked whether he could attend the meeting.

## Pronouns and What They Refer To (p. 102)

1. his or her
2. his
3. its
4. their
5. my

## Pronouns (Showing Ownership or Belonging To) (p. 102)

1. hers
2. theirs
3. Its
4. Their
5. His

## The Words *Each, Either . . . Or,* and *Neither . . . Nor* (p. 102)

You should have a line under the following.
1. has
2. is
3. are
4. has
5. knows

## Adjectives and Adverbs (p. 103)

1. young; loudly
2. best; faster
3. taller; quickly
4. oldest; here
5. old; completely

## Regular and Irregular Verbs (p. 103)

1. learned, has learned, is learning
2. cried, has cried, is crying
3. cut, has cut, is cutting
4. spoke, has spoken, is speaking
5. wrote, has written, is writing

## Using the Words *Has* and *Have* with Verbs (p. 103)

1. have put
2. bets
3. cost
4. have bet
5. put

## The Verbs *Cut, Cuts, Will Cut, Has Cut, Have Cut,* and *Had Cut* (p. 104)

1. cut
2. will cut
3. have cut
4. will cut
5. has cut

## The Verbs *Set* and *Sit* (p. 104)

1. set
2. Sit
3. will set
4. set
5. sat

## The Words *Can* and *May* (p. 104)

1. can
2. May
3. Can
4. can
5. May

## The Verbs *Let* and *Leave* (p. 104)

1. Let
2. leave
3. let
4. left
5. let

## The Words *Your* and *You're*, *Its* and *It's*, *Their* and *They're*, and *Whose* and *Who's* (p. 105)

1. Who's
2. Whose
3. You're
4. It's
5. Their

## The Comma (p. 105)

1. My beautiful, precious child hurt herself before.
2. NC
3. The long, slimy worm crawled across the floor.
4. NC
5. This loud, noisy party is getting on my nerves.

## Verb Forms as Adjectives (p. 105)

1. crying
2. talking
3. running
4. working
5. flying

## Nouns as Adjectives (pp. 105–106)

You should have a line under the following.

1. storm
2. kitchen
3. chicken
4. steel
5. football

## Misplaced Descriptive Words (p. 106)

1. Diane, eating a pear, drove her car.
2. The carpenter, chewing gum, fixed the window.
3. George, scratching his head, sat in a chair.
4. Patrick, wearing shorts, went into the store.
5. Dave, carrying a newspaper, left the train.

## Unnecessary Words (p. 106)

1. Please take those shoes off the bed.
2. The men went out the door just a moment ago.
3. We need to buy a half pound of cheese.
4. Fred lives near me off Broad Street.
5. I will not wait longer than half an hour for you.

## Double Negatives (p. 107)

1. I don't understand anything.
2. Pablo didn't do anything.
3. Nobody knows anything here.
4. The police don't say anything.
5. This butter isn't any good anymore.

## Contractions (p. 107)

1. who's
2. we're
3. there's
4. what's
5. it'll
6. we'll
7. let's
8. they've
9. she's
10. you're

## The Words *A* and *An* (p. 107)

1. a heavy load
2. an honorable man
3. an iron-clad alibi
4. an aspirin
5. a bank
6. an argument
7. an eager person
8. an earthquake
9. an unclaimed ticket
10. a cracker

## Writing Paragraphs (p. 108)

You should have a line under the following words.

The sex-education course at my children's junior high school delivers a well-balanced survey of important issues. On one hand, the course gives careful attention to the pleasures and benefits of an intimate sexual relationship. On the other, it cautions about the dangers of irresponsible sex, especially in this day and age. I am glad my children enjoy the course, and I hope it helps them develop attitudes toward sex that makes it a positive part of their lives.

## Organizing Sentences into a Paragraph (p. 108)

You should have written the following:

Mario did all but one of the tasks of his job well. He handled the switchboard with ease, entered data into the computer accurately, and dealt well with customers. However, his failing was that he didn't keep his supervisor informed about important events. One day his supervisor made a decision that turned out to be very embarrassing. She made the mistake only because Mario had not told her about the change in a certain customer's order. As a result, Mario was put on warning and advised to be careful to relay critical information to his supervisor.

## Sentence Variety (p. 109)

Sample paragraph:

I will never forget how I met my wife. One day, when I was working as a cash register clerk in a food store, she came into the store with her mother to buy things. When I saw her, I fell in love with her right away. I was delighted when her mother came to my check-out lane. I tried to act very cool, and I smiled at both of them. Then they left the store. I was upset because I felt I would never see the girl of my dreams again. However, two days later a friend invited me to a party. You can imagine my surprise when I saw the girl of my dreams there. I went up to her and said, "Hi." I reminded her that I had seen her before in the food store, and the rest is history.

## Proofreading (p. 109)

This is the paragraph as you should have written it. The words and punctuation that were changed are in dark type.

Whenever my friend, his brother, and I would walk down the street, we always tried to avoid stepping on the cracks of the sidewalk. No one ever said that we shouldn't, but we just didn't. Once, my little sister, who always liked to follow us, ran in front of us. Then she purposely stepped on every crack in the sidewalk. Somehow, my friend, his brother, and I felt that our luck changed after that. I know it sounds silly, but nothing went right for us for a long time.

## Writing an Invitation (p. 110)

Sample letter:

```
                          August 1, 1990
Dear James,

   I am having a little get-together
at my house on Saturday, August 20, at
8:00 P.M. I am inviting our whole gang,
so it should be lots of fun.
   Please phone by August 15 to let me
know if you can make it. I really hope
you can. My number is 555-9870.

                       Your friend,
                       Sally
```

## Writing a Business Letter (p. 111)

Sample letter:

```
                     411 Hooper Avenue
                     Trenton, New Jersey 08618
                     September 2, 1990

New Jersey State Department of Labor
234 East State Street
Trenton, New Jersey 08618

Dear Sir:

   I applied six weeks ago to receive my
sick-pay benefits. However, I still
have not received any checks from your
office. I am still home ill and need
the money to pay my bills. I phoned,
but I was told to write a letter and
send it to your office.
   Please find out what happened to my
checks.

                     Yours truly,
                     Michael Brown
```

## Spelling (p. 112)

| | | |
|---|---|---|
| 1. reason | 8. argument | 15. recognize |
| 2. matter | 9. believe | 16. opinion |
| 3. exercise | 10. necessary | 17. company |
| 4. length | 11. succeed | 18. calendar |
| 5. lonely | 12. building | 19. corner |
| 6. position | 13. expensive | 20. schedule |
| 7. accident | 14. height | |

## Alphabetizing (Using the Dictionary) (p. 112)

1. Yes    2. Yes    3. Yes    4. Yes    5. Yes